Favorite Story-Poems
of Maine's Unique Storyteller
Gaylon "Jeep" Wilcox,
The Woodland Bard

Gaylon "Jeep" Wilcox

Edited by Margaret Yocom

Liongrass Editions
2018

Copyright © 2018 by Gaylon "Jeep" Wilcox
All Rights Reserved

Except for brief quotations in critical reviews or articles,
no part of this book may be reproduced in any manner
without the prior written permission of the copyright holder.

Maine's Unique Storyteller
Jeep Wilcox —The Woodland Bard
P.O. Box 653
Rangeley, Maine 04970
207–864–5260

ISBN 978-0-578-42280-0

Library of Congress Control Number: 2018965349

Design by Höhne-Werner Design of Wilton, Maine
www.heyneon.com

This book was designed using Adobe Caslon and Nueva Std typefaces.

Printed by Walch Printing of Portland, Maine

Cover photograph of Gaylon "Jeep" Wilcox at Steep Bank Pool in
the Kennebago River, courtesy of Jeep Wilcox.

DEDICATION

I would like to dedicate this book to folklorist Dr. Margaret Yocom, affectionately known as "Peggy," for without her expertise it never would have become a reality. My scant schooling days of long ago left me a stranger in the land of modern technology, lacking skills needed to compensate. Peggy's uncanny ability to turn over stones revealing hidden treasures and to recognize diamonds in rough form—coupled with relentless determination to bring to fruition what most can't see—is what makes her stand out as one of a kind. While sharing her expertise to bring this book to be for many to enjoy, she also shared with me a friendship second to none.

Peggy and Jeep on Saddleback Mountain.

PRAISE FOR JEEP WILCOX'S STORY-POEMS

Jeep is highly attuned to the natural world and the culture of the woodsman. His innate ability to communicate this to an audience in an entertaining way is what makes him so special.
—Kirby Holcombe, Columnist, *Northwoods Sporting Journal*

Jeep understands the spirit of the North Woods and shares his insights with those of us who need to hear.
—Nan Turner Waldron (1912–2000), author of *North Woods Walkabout* and *Journey to the Outermost House*

We are very fortunate and delighted to have Jeep Wilcox perform here entertaining our bus tour visitors. He gives our people a true sense of Maine and the Rangeley area.
—Ed and Fay Carpenter, former owners of the Rangeley Inn

Each story that Jeep tells is introduced by a bit of wit and reflection, one leading into the other in an even flow of philosophy, humor, and occasional leg pulling. Just as an artist paints a picture with oils, Jeep paints a picture with humor, wit, and style.
—Shelly Poulin, Journalist, *Original Irregular*, Kingfield

Jeep Wilcox's reputation as a storyteller par excellence is well established in Rangeley and the rest of the State of Maine.
—Ann Whitney, Journalist

The world loves to hear a good story, and good stories, not to mention good storytellers, acquire polish like a rough rock smoothed by the sea into a beach pebble. We have one of those smooth pebbles in our midst—Gaylon "Jeep" Wilcox. Jeep has been authenticated as a traditional storyteller by Edward D. "Sandy" Ives (1925-2009), folklorist at the University of Maine and founder of the Northeast Archives of Folklore and Oral History. Ives is world-renowned as a folklorist and served for many years as president of the American Folklore Society. In his account of traditional storytellers, Ives finds that so-called "tradition bearers" draw upon their native culture for their strength and material, [as Jeep does]. There is something almost religious about Jeep's famous scenic photographs and poems [that depict the beauty of the Rangeley Region]. *Rangeley Highlander*, 1/9/1997.
—George Chappell, Journalist, English teacher, author of two books of poetry

Jeep is a storyteller in the classic sense, a transmitter of tradition that has no written basis. His stories serve as curtain-raisers for his poems. Even his prose is poetic.
—Dan Behrman (1924-1990), Writer-Editor for UNESCO, contributor to *The New York Times*

I have been fortunate to see Jeep weave wonderful storytelling performances for students of various ages and grades. It has not ceased to amaze me at how he is able to get both student and teacher alike so completely within his frame of reference and keep them interactively involved through his performance.
—Gary Crook, former Principal of Rangeley Lakes Regional School, 1993

Jeep Wilcox is a storyteller with a twist. His storytelling is just pure, from the heart, down home Rangeley, Maine—as he'll joyously tell you in his slow and gentle winding, flowing way. It's that turn of his smile that keeps you guessing: truth or tale? He quickened my dead spirit to want to write again. That is true Power and Beauty!
—Barbara van Soeren, former 4th grade teacher, Rangeley Lakes Regional School, 1993

As a summer resident of Rangeley, Maine, I have known Gaylon "Jeep" Wilcox for many years. I have heard him regale countless visitors to the area, speaking in a Maine accent thick enough to cut, with stories of life in the tiny community as it is and used to be. As a travel journalist who has crisscrossed the United States and explored more than 70 other countries around the world, I have concluded that despite their cultural, social, and countless other differences, people everywhere are basically very much the same in many ways. Jeep elegantly and humorously captures and depicts the essence of the folks who live in his small, rather isolated town. In doing so, he also expresses in very human, down-to-earth terms the common desires and dreams that are shared by people around the world.
—Victor Block, Society of American Travel Writers, Washington, DC, and Rangeley, Maine

Jeep's work has been compared to that of Garrison Keillor of Lake Wobegon fame, a pure down-to-earth common man.
—Kimberly Dolbier, former general manager and editor, *The Rangeley Highlander*

JEEP WILCOX'S SELECTED APPEARANCES, PUBLICATIONS, AND HONORS

c. 1952. Jeep Wilcox publishes a story-poem for the first time. In *The Rangeley Record.*

Summer 1975. Jeep performs at the Rangeley Inn for the first time. Owners Ed and Faye Carpenter ask him to tell his stories for a bus tour staying at the Inn. From now on, Jeep performs countless times for Rangeley organizations such as the Garden Club, Logging Museum, Rotary, Shriners, and many families' reunions. He also performs multiple times in Phillips, ME, at such organizations as the Community Center, local churches, Old Home Days, and Shadagee Seniors Housing.

Early 1980s. *Lewiston Sun Journal* publishes Dave Karkos' article that includes "Are Fairy Tales Real?"

July 17, 1981. *The Rangeley Highlander* publishes Jeep's story-poem "The Mad Whittler" in their article "A Little Wild Mountain Poetry."

Summers of 1981-1986. Jeep performs at the Maine Festival.

August 3, 1987. Jeep appears in the Channel 5 Boston television program "The Chronicle," in their "On the Road Again" segment, with host Peter Mehegan.

July 19, 1988. Jeep performs at the Rangeley Lakes Region Historical Society's Annual Meeting, Oscar Riddle, President. He gives two of his framed photos and story-poems for their Building fund auction. Jeep performs many more times for the Historical Society, including their Annual Potluck Dinner on June 17, 1993.

December 31, 1988. Jeep performs at Maine Arts' "New Year's Eve Portland."

October 1989. Jeep performs at Upcountry Artists gallery in Kingfield, ME.

October 7, 1990. Jeep performs in Bethel, ME, sponsored by Mahoosuc Arts.

June 1991. *The Original Irregular* publishes "Jeep Wilcox brings area meanderings to his stories" by Carol Engan in their *Rangeley Area Summertime Guide* (p. 5).

July 26-28, 1991. Jeep performs during the Lowell Folk Festival in Lowell, MA.

June 1994. The graduating seniors of the Rangeley school publish "Special People In Our Lives" in *The Tattler, Yearbook of Rangeley Lakes Regional School* (p. 3).

August 2, 1997. Jeep performs at the Maine Festival, Thomas Point Beach, during the Maine Storytellers Convention on the Traditions Stage, along with John McDonald, Michael Parent, Jo Radner, and others.

Fall 1997. Jeep performs at the Pine Tree State Locksmith Association's convention at By-the-Sea, in Belfast, ME.

June 1999. *The Rangeley Highlander* publishes Jeep's story-poem "Children On Parade" in its seasonal booklet "This Summer In Rangeley" (p. 19). *The Highlander* republishes this story-poem regularly, in honor of the Children's Day Parade in Rangeley on the Third of July.

July 1999. Jeep is one of the featured artists in "Working the Woods," the exhibit by folklorists Margaret Yocom and Kathleen Mundell, funded by the Maine Arts Commission. Opens during the Logging Festival of the Rangeley Lakes Region Logging Museum where Margaret Yocom serves as curator.

July 7, 2000. Jeep is one of the featured traditional artists in the exhibit "Gather 'Round: Tales of New England's Work-A-Day World" by Vermont Folklife Center, Middlebury, VT. Margaret Yocom conducted the fieldwork for Jeep's participation in the exhibit.

2000. Margaret Yocom and Jeep's co-authored essay, " 'Just Call Me Sandy, Son': Poet Jeep Wilcox's Tribute to Sandy Ives," is published by the University of Maine Press in *Northeast Folklore: Essays in Honor of Edward D. Ives*, edited by Pauleena MacDougall and David Taylor (pp. 405-414).

2002. Jeep performs at the Northwest Folklife Festival, Seattle, WA, along with woodcarver Rodney Richard, Sr., and other traditional artists from the northeast in the "Northeast Meets Northwest" festival section, co-curated by Margaret Yocom.

August 2002. Jeep performs at the National Folk Festival, Bangor, ME.

December 20, 2002. *The Rangeley Highlander* publishes "Born To Fly," Jeep's tribute to pilot Stephen Bean who died in a plane crash near Rangeley (p. 6).

September 16, 2003. Jeep performs at the Open House and Kick-Off of the Gold LEAF Institute Senior College at the University of Maine, Farmington.

August 2005. Jeep loans his exhibit "Jeep Wilcox's Poetry and Photography" to the Rangeley Lakes Region Logging Museum. (See *The Rangeley Highlander* photograph by Margaret Yocom, 2 September 2005).

August 2, 2006. Jeep is an honoree at the Second Annual Literary Gala of the Rangeley Public Library.

2011. Maine Folklife Center of the University of Maine, Orono, launches its "Maine Song and Story Sampler" website that features songs and stories from across the state, including Jeep's story-poems "The Mad Whittler" and "Man Made Lake." In 2013, the Center publishes these materials in *Northeast Folklore XLV.* https://umaine.edu/folklife/maine-song-story-sampler

August 5-6, 2011. Jeep is a featured storyteller at the first Western Maine Storytelling Festival, Farmington, ME, along with Jackson Gilman and Michael Parent.

December 9, 2011. Kimberley Dolbier publishes "Rangeley Storyteller celebrates 30 years of entertaining" about Jeep in *The Rangeley Highlander* (p. 15).

November 2012. *The Rangeley Highlander* publishes Jeep's story-poem "Winter Blues" in their *Winter Guide*, p. 16.

November 2014. Kirby Holcombe publishes Jeep's story-poem "Lying Mountain Lion" in his article of the same name, in the *Northwoods Sporting Journal* (Vol. 21:11, pp. 78-79). Holcombe suggests that although mountain lions may not live in Maine, they do travel through Maine and have been spotted by himself and others.

July 2014. Jeep is named Poet Laureate of the Rangeley Lakes Region Logging Museum and performs during the Opening Ceremonies of the Museum's Logging Festival.

September 9, 2014. Jeep performs at the Rangeley Public Library, Rangeley. Brian Ellis video-records his performance for the Rangeley Lakes Historical Society's archive.

June 16, 2015. Jeep performs at the Rangeley Inn for a bus tour from Perkiomen, PA.

July 20, 2015. Jeep performs at the New Vineyard Public Library, New Vineyard, ME.

July 24, 2015. Jeep is inducted into the Logger's Hall of Fame of the Rangeley Lakes Region Logging Museum, having been nominated the previous summer by a committee of loggers.

September 13, 2015. Jeep performs at the Rangeley Public Library.

September 8, 2017. *The Rangeley Highlander* publishes "'Jeep' Wilcox Honors His Brother on POW/MIA Recognition Day" which includes Jeep's story-poem "The Missing One" (p. 16). Also published in *The Lewiston Sun Journal,* September 15.

BOOK POWER

Long before today's world of electronics and modern technology such as computers and smart phones, a valuable means of education and entertainment was a good book. As time passed and new techniques were developed, the importance of the book started to decline—though it was not forgotten. In the world of electronics, things change so rapidly that today's next big thing is tomorrow's history.

A downside of electronics is not only does it require energy of some kind, it can invade the privacy of your inner peace, as well as that of those around you. While electronics come and go, a book is forever. The pages may yellow with age, but its contents remain the same and can be enjoyed anywhere, at any time desired. It can pass time while traveling by plane or bus—as well as occupy your mind as you spend time in waiting rooms for the many requirements in life. It can be placed on a stand beside the bed, allowing you to read a paragraph at your leisure, then momentarily close your eyes and escape from reality.

Book power takes us on journeys to faraway places by joining us with its text. For those who seek tranquility, a book will always be cherished. Books are forever.

—Jeep Wilcox

COMMON-FOLK POETRY

Poetry has had a tendency to become the property of the highly educated. There are poets and physicians, both, who honestly believe that "diaphoretic and tremulous" is a better way of saying "sweaty and shaky," leaving many common folks with smaller vocabularies unable to understand.

Our world today is very rich in beautiful poetry created by the best poets in the land, but many people cannot grasp it, due to meager educations such as mine. Poetry is one of man's oldest forms of literature, with narrative poetry having been around for centuries, telling stories of heroes, villains, love and death, as well as the mysteries of life, real or imaginary—poems that tell a story where the author can describe scenes, people, and even feelings vividly. This type of poetry was first written by people with scant educations, so the language used is simple to understand, making it sound very much like the way we all speak in conversation—yet it is still poetry, giving meaning to what I call "common-folk poetry."

The popularity of poems is on the rise, with a national movement to return the language of poetry to all of us—to people who go to work and drive trucks, or "flip burgers," or work in the construction trade. With a less than average education, without any schooling in writing, I shy away from the label of "poet," preferring the title of "storyteller," allowing me the freedom to create with feelings from deep within heart and soul.

—Jeep Wilcox

TABLE OF CONTENTS

Everything In Life Is A Story 12
I Climb A Mountain 16
The Fool's Gold 20
Reflections 24
Man Made Lake 28
Smokey's Home 34
A Real Native: The Boot From L.L. Bean 38
The Spirit Tree 46
Children's Day Parade 50
The Giving Tree 54
School Inspirations: From Tree To Table 58
School Inspirations: A Moment's Worth 62
School Inspirations: Special People In Our Lives 66
School Inspirations: I See 70
The Mad Whittler 74
Are Fairy Tales Real? 80
Brother Of The Bear 84
Walks Of Life 90
The Missing One 94
Beauty All Around 100
Seeing Is Believing 104
Deer Mountain Run 108
The Eighth Day 112
Born To Fly 118
Winter Blues 124
Nature's Way 128
Noah's Mistake 132
The Lying Mountain Lion 138
The Logger Who Cuts The Tree 142
A Legend Of The Weeping Willow Tree 146
Local Entertainment Center 150
    Rangeley Logging Man 152
    The Devil's Machine 154
    John Devil Reforms? 156
    Blue Mack Blues 158
    The Wagon Wheel 160
You Can't Get There From Here,
But You Can Get Here From There 162

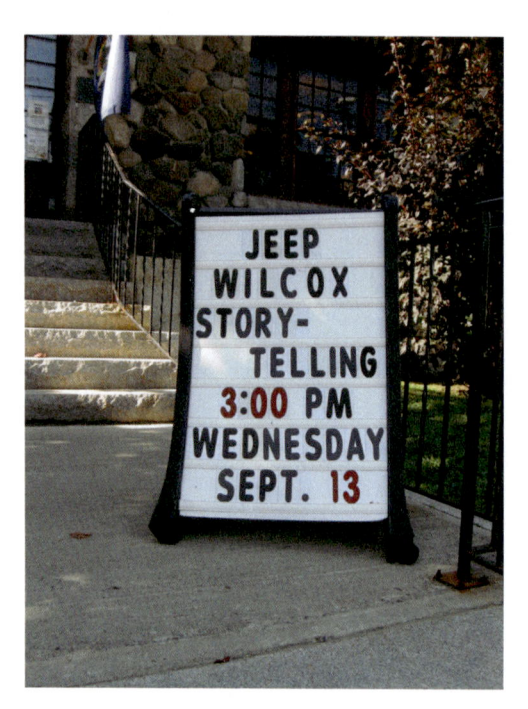

At the Rangeley Public Library.

EVERYTHING IN LIFE IS A STORY

The stories I write come to me in many ways and at different times. At times, a story will come to mind so fast, I will grab the first thing I see to write on; and, so as not to lose the concentration, I write so rapidly I can hardly read my own writing after the "passing." Other times, thoughts or verses come to me at different times, sort of piece-meal; and I jot them down on a piece of scrap paper and let them collect in my shirt pocket. Strangely enough, I have had the endings of stories come to me first and the beginnings come last. I just sort of go along, ignoring any system, and let them collect in my pocket, for it never fails—at the right time, a little bell will ring in my head telling me a story has come together and that it's time for me to take a minute to put it all together and make it happen.

One problem I do have is—as I get up in the morning to go to work, and it's time to go to the closet to get a clean shirt, I forget to clean the pockets out of the dirty one. Well, my wife will do the laundry, and she doesn't clean out my pockets, either. She takes my dirty shirt with my precious notes still in the pocket and throws it into the washing machine, and I end up with a pile of soggy, ink-stained paper that is impossible to read.

One day at work a thought came to me, and I quickly grabbed a piece of scrap paper to write it down; and, as I started to put it in my pocket, immediately a little bell went off, alerting me to take a minute and put the story together. As I dug into my pocket, I realized that I had put on a clean shirt that morning, and I sort of panicked at a vision of my wife taking wet, soggy paper out of the washing machine.

At the end of the day as I hurried home, I kind of held my breath, hoping that just once my wife had cleaned out the pockets before she put my shirt in the washing machine. I rushed in the house, but no such luck. There on the counter top was a pile of wet, soggy paper—and the wrong kind of ending to my precious story.

I just couldn't help it. The hollers and bellows just poured out of me. I bawled my wife out something fierce. I said, "I just don't understand! You've been my wife for well over forty years, and you know I don't clean my shirt pockets out. It's your job and your duty to clean my pockets out before you put my shirt in the washing machine!" I chewed her out for a good ten minutes. As I stopped long enough to catch my breath, she just looked at me and grinned, and said, "Look at it like this, dear. Thanks to me, no one can accuse you of writing dirty stories!"

Well, my stories don't get censored, but they sure do get laundered every now and then. I calmed down very quickly, for I decided I would rather write another story than I would search for another wife.

Some of my stories are based on true experiences, some are based on experiences that aren't quite true, and some are based on experiences that aren't true at all! Anyone who reads or listens to them has to be their own judge and try to put them in the category where they think they belong. The amazing thing is, some could fit any or all of the categories. In fact, there are times I'm not sure myself just which one they belong in.

Everything In Life Is A Story

Everything in life is a story,
be it a person, place, or thing.
And even if I tune them out,
I hear these stories ring.

I do not go searching.
At times, I try not to see.
But for some unknown reason,
these stories keep searching for me.

They say, "Too long we've been silent.
We now need to be told.
Please, Jeep, be our teller.
Make us now unfold.

"Some of us will be humorous
some, a little blue.
But, in the way you tell us—
we'll leave that up to you."

So I just accept my fate.
The tales will sound at last.
Many from the present
and some from days gone past.

For I vow to tell these stories
just as I hear them cry.
And I'll tell them to all of you
until my pen runs dry.

Jeep on Saddleback Mountain. The higher the mountain, the closer to Heaven.

I CLIMB A MOUNTAIN

Reaching into the sky to over 4,000 feet at its summit, Saddleback Mountain is one of the most rugged mountains in western Maine. Most people know that the Appalachian Trail traverses this mountain, and they know that there's a ski resort on one of its slopes, but that is the equivalent of a drop of water in a bucketful compared to the many wonders that Saddleback holds—wonders of pleasure and wonders of misery that never fade from memory once you've experienced them.

For those born to fish, casting a fly upon the waters of a remote mountain pond to catch a native pink-bellied trout—the silence broken with an occasional slap of a beaver's tail hitting the water in warning—is a pleasure worthy of remembering. For those who enjoy the centuries old Maine tradition of hunting the elusive whitetail deer in hopes of outwitting a trophy-sized buck and joining the prestigious "Biggest Bucks in Maine Club"—that is another memorable pleasure. And for those hikers who wander the ridges and valleys of this mountain that deserves the title "God's Country," stopping to slake their thirst with cool, crystal clear, sweet water from a babbling mountain stream with the constant smell of balsam riding the whispering breeze—that is a pleasure indeed.

This same mountain, though, with its history of logging that goes back hundreds of years and is still being done today, can produce many miseries as well. For those of us who worked at the logger's trade in the past, battling the elements for a wage so paltry that a poverty wage would be considered a raise, Saddleback has also produced memories that are more like nightmares. Floundering in waist-deep snow during sub-zero temperatures, working every day with the hazards of felling trees, and facing the frigid water of the early spring river drives filled us with so many miseries that new cuss words were invented every day.

As my youth waned and senior years slowed me down, my family grew concerned about my safety during my many solitary wanderings on Saddleback Mountain. They feared I could be injured by slipping or falling on the rough terrain, and they didn't want me to make the trek alone anymore. The sweet part of my bittersweet memories remains, though; and my urge to climb the mountain still exists. Each year when my birthday rolls around, my kids strive to give me something I really want; and I always say, "Climb the mountain with me." They point out that having spent a lifetime on Saddleback, I already know the pleasures, the miseries, and all the secrets this mountain holds; so why, they ask, do I still insist on climbing it?

I Climb A Mountain

I climb a high mountain,
not for the view.
I needed a feeling
of being closer to You.

I give thanks, Heavenly Father,
for this life on Earth You gave.
When it's over, I pray,
my soul You will save.

May the four winds carry
to You these words I say—
I climb a high mountain
to bow head and pray.

When it is time for me
to leave this world behind,
I pray to be blessed
by You, so divine.

Grant entrance to Your kingdom,
wash away all my sin,
place Your arm around me
and welcome me in.

Oh, I climb a high mountain
to give thanks and pray, too,
for a life everlasting
in Heaven with You.

A fool and his gold are parted.

THE FOOL'S GOLD

As a small boy in school, I used to think that the first gold ever discovered in America was out West, during the gold rush days. As I got older and learned more about the State of Maine and my hometown of Rangeley, I was amazed to learn a little-known fact: the truth is that one of the very first known discoveries of gold anywhere in Maine was found in a stream that flows down from Saddleback Mountain right here in Rangeley.

At first, I found it hard to believe, but think about it: Maine and New England were discovered and settled long before the wagons went west. People found gold here, but nowhere near enough to create a gold rush. At the time, the value and amount of gold found here were so small, it was not practical to bother with it, but it certainly enriched the history of my hometown.

Another place gold was discovered in the early days of settling Rangeley was in a stream known as the Swift River. Swift River originates high on a mountain in the Rangeley Lakes Region and tumbles down the mountainside through Coos Canyon in Byron as it joins other waters on its way to the sea.

In the Coos Canyon area now, there are outfitters who supply knowledge and equipment to many vacationers and visitors who wish to experience a romantic, long-ago thrill in a search for gold. Some people have even gotten expert enough that they do quite well panning for gold in Swift River year 'round. Occasionally, a news headline tells of someone stumbling on a fair-sized nugget.

I find it very interesting, too, just how it was that gold was first discovered in Swift River. In the early days of the Rangeley settlement, it was routine for a settler or a farmer to build on a lakeshore or a riverbank, for water. One farmer built himself a farm on the banks of Swift River.

Of course, on a farm, there are all kinds of animals, and a farm isn't a farm without hens and chickens. Now, a hen is a type of critter that has a thing in its throat called a crop. It is a sack-like enlargement of the hen's gullet, and a hen stores grit in it to help grind up its food before digestion. If you have ever seen a hen in a hen yard pecking at the ground, and nothing there for it to eat, chances are that hen is picking fine pieces of grit out of the soil to store in its crop. Hens have the skill of picking just the right-sized pieces of grit to do the job.

Now, this farmer had a very large flock of hens; and to keep foxes and other wild animals away from them, he cooped them up in a pen. As time went by, the hens had taken all of the usable grit from the soil; and they started having problems digesting their food. The farmer realized what the problem was, and his solution was very simple. He shoveled gravel from the riverbed into the hen pen; and the hens, of course, were able to pick out just the right-sized pieces of grit.

Typical of farm life, the farmer had a routine: every Sunday, he would butcher a hen or two and have chicken for his Sunday dinner. One Sunday while he was dressing off a hen, he discovered a small gold nugget in the hen's crop. Recalling the gravel he had shoveled out of the riverbed, he ran to the river; and while he was poking around, he found more gold. That was how the gold in Swift River was discovered.

Every now and then I think of that ole farmer, and I can't help but feel a little sorry for him. If he hadn't have killed that hen, sooner or later he might have had a hen that laid a golden egg!

I used to believe that gold was always yellow, bright, and shiny. Over the years, I've learned that gold can come in many different colors and shapes, sometimes embedded in ore that is unrecognizable as gold by someone the likes of me. In all the years and miles that I have wandered Saddleback Mountain, one thing that I have learned is the true meaning of "fool's gold." It happened this way:

The Fool's Gold

I was hiking Saddleback Mountain,
which I often do.
I sat down on a boulder,
just to enjoy the view.

As I was admiring the scenery
with my scanning eyes,
I started tossing pebbles
that seemed heavy for their size.

They were scattered on a ledge
that stuck out kind of flat
as though they tumbled from a pocket
of that boulder where I sat.

When I went to bed that night,
sleep I could not find.
Those strange pebbles I'd been tossing
kept floating through my mind.

So I opened an encyclopedia,
and there the truth was told.
Those funny little pebbles
contained nuggets of gold!

For years now, I've been searching
for where I sat that day.
In my hands I held a fortune,
and I threw it all away.

Soon I'll quit that mountain,
for my bones are getting old.
But scattered up there is a fortune—
a fortune in this fool's gold.

Small's Falls.

REFLECTIONS

Since the very beginning, one of the most impressive spectacles of nature is the waterfall. Surely, Adam and Eve at one time or another must have sat on a rock at the bottom of a waterfall somewhere enjoying such a scenic wonder. The State of Maine has many pristine waterfalls that clearly document the State's pure, crystal clear waters.

One such waterfall lies beside the eastern gateway to the Rangeley Lakes Region, off Route 4, just south of Saddleback Mountain. Its name of "Small's Falls" is very misleading, for it is far from being small. A more appropriate name might be something like "Wonder Falls." It is believed that many years ago when the Region was first settled, a settler with the family name of Small built a homestead by the river; and after the passing of many, many years, it is still known as Small's Falls. I know of an old stone foundation which appears to have been built with river rocks, not far from the Falls, and I often wonder if it could be the site.

Small's Falls is created as the Sandy River tumbles down over a massive ledge of rock through a spectacular gorge. If a poll was taken to decide the most beautiful waterfall in Maine, I believe Small's Falls would definitely be the winner.

As years went by and the tract of land where the Falls are located changed hands from one family to another, it was presented to the State of Maine and is now a very clean, well-maintained roadside rest area to be enjoyed by all. By today's standards, if this site were privately owned, it would probably be fenced off and a fee would be charged to enjoy it. Truly, it is one of the most generous and beautiful gifts the State of Maine has ever received. With the exception of a small wooden foot bridge to allow crossing the stream and a couple of steel safety fences high above the sheer walls of the canyon, the area still has its original wilderness beauty of long ago. Over the years, the fame of Small's Falls has spread far and wide, and it attracts visitors, photographers, and artists from well beyond the State of Maine's borders. Now that weddings are often held in many places other than a church, Small's Falls has become a popular spot for such occasions.

As a young boy, I remember my family and neighbors getting together and spending a day of rest and recreation at Small's Falls. No, everybody didn't have a car then. Some old farmer would have a hay truck or something. Half a dozen families would jump onto the truck, and we would drive down to Small's Falls. We'd spend the day having a cookout—or just having a grand old day. And everybody got a big enjoyment out of just being at Small's Falls.

I have spent many hours of my time at the Falls when it was completely deserted, enjoying the solitude; and I would get so wrapped up in the spell it cast on me, I would lose all sense of time.

One time I was there sitting on a rock and gazing into the plunge pool at the bottom of the Falls when a thought passed through my mind: "Imagine all the people who have stopped here over the years from all walks of life." I started to see their reflections shimmering on the surface of the water:

Reflections

Honeymooners tossing pennies,
as they make a wish.
Fathers holding fish poles,
teaching sons to fish.

Mothers showing babies,
while they gossip there,
and little children wading,
splashing water everywhere.

Family clans a-gathering
to share a barbeque.
Young lovers holding hands,
whispering "I love you."

Old folks reminiscing
or dozing in the sun.
Weary travelers resting,
wishing day was done.

Forget-me-nots a-blooming
near the water where it's cool—
all are many reflections
I've seen in Small's Falls pool.

OLD FLAGSTAFF—1950

According to Flagstaff historian Kenny Wing, the buildings in this postcard photo were owned by his great-uncle Alvin Wing and by Mae Savage, who, when this photograph was taken in 1950, were in a legal dispute with Central Maine Power over the purchase price of their properties. Wing and Savage had agreed on a purchase price with CMP in the 1940s; but, in 1949, CMP claimed that their properties were worth less because of the destruction of the village to create Flagstaff Lake.

MAN MADE LAKE

A constant in life is change. The only thing that remains the same is—everything changes. Changes of happenstance by God or Mother Nature and Father Time are uncontrollable by mankind who must accept and adapt to them in life.

Changes made by man are of a different nature. Some benefit many or just a few; some changes are a result of a hare-brained fiasco that should have never happened. Only the passage of time can tell if the change is for better or worse.

Once upon a time there was a land with a lush green valley surrounded by mountains heavily forested with old-growth, virgin timber. The valley floor was layered with fertile soil, with a cold-water river meandering through, making it very rich farmland. Nature's abundance of flora and fauna added to the richness of the valley. In the year 1911, the *Maine Woods Magazine* described it as the country where the best hunting and fishing in America existed.

Nestled in this valley was a close-knit community of three villages. The village of Dead River was named for the river itself, for being cold and slow-moving. The villages of Bigelow and Flagstaff derived their names from a story. In 1775, Benedict Arnold rested his army on his march to attack Quebec City, and Major Timothy Bigelow climbed a mountain to see if he could see the city of Quebec; a flagstaff was erected there. The region became commonly known as Flagstaff.

The inhabitants of the valley were mostly generations of settlers from the early 1800s. Peace and happiness ruled the land. Then came change.

Founders of Central Maine Power Company (CMP) designed a plan to dam up the Dead River, and the Kennebec

Reservoir Company (KRC) was incorporated to control the waterways of the mighty Kennebec River on its journey seaward, to create a man-made lake, three miles wide by 24 miles long, spanning over 20,000 acres. In 1918, CMP offered to buy land and houses from those willing to sell and move away, but there were very few takers; most felt a project of this magnitude—being so unnecessary—could never come to be. Some worry started when, in 1923, the State Legislature granted CMP permission to dam up the river. Then, in 1927, a dark cloud settled over the valley. The Legislature granted CMP permission to take possession of land and homes by eminent domain; it gave CMP the power to take private property at prices far below the true value of appraisal, leaving owners with no say or choice. Either move or wish you had.

In 1948, I was one of a 1,000-man crew "cutting flowage"—strip cutting and burning brush—clearing the land to make Flagstaff Lake. The wages I earned helped put food on the table but filled my heart and soul with sadness. With the State of Maine boasting 6,000 lakes and ponds and 32,000 miles of rivers and streams, I failed to see the need to destroy a touch of Heaven on Earth to make another lake. What a sorrowful feeling—seeing so many 100-year-old New England homesteads still standing strong being burned, many with furnishings still inside for lack of a place to start anew. And, seeing some homes being razed, trying to salvage enough to start elsewhere if time permitted before the flood. It was so sad to see some livestock being killed off due to nowhere to go.

Being a drought-stricken time with the State of Maine losing thousands of acres of prime forestland to wildfires, it was frightening to see so many runaway blazes so fierce that it gave insight to what it would be like gazing into the valley of Hell. It was heart-breaking to see over 300 graves dug up, with the remains being moved to a different location. It disturbed the contractors doing the moving so much they took money from their own pockets and purchased a second-hand hearse to add a little dignity to the process. Overall, it gave a little understanding to how the Native Americans must have felt when the wagons went west.

A few years later as I was proudly serving my country in the United States Army, I found myself on a lonely outpost in a foreign country on guard duty, providing security to a piece of America's best—an F86 Sabre jet. Thinking of folks back home, I saw the irony of it all: while doing my part to help keep them free, they were victims of eminent domain. Flagstaff Lake is presently a recreational resource enjoyed by residents and tourists alike; but for those who know, it all came at a terrible price and is known as a forgotten land.

Man Made Lake

I'll never forget the day
they took my home away,
to make a lake that God did not plan.
Though it has been many years,
I still recall the tears
shed when they made Flagstaff Dam.

My only choice made me sad—
either move or wish I had.
No way could I stop their flood.
So knowing nothing I could do,
using a token dollar or two,
they took what cost me sweat and blood.

From Eustis Ridge I see
man's lake of misery,
where once I tilled the fertile sod.
'Twas there I made my stand,
trying to convince my fellow man
to leave the lake-building up to God.

Yes, my life still goes on,
but for me dreams are gone,
haunted with nightmares from days gone by.
Like a vagabond, I still roam,
for the day they took away my home
was the day my dreams began to die.

Someday I'll pass on,
and from this land I'll be gone.
Inside of Heaven's gate I'll stand.
Once again I'll shed a tear
for all of those still here,
with roots in a forgotten land.

FIRE DANGER
MODERATE
TODAY!
PREVENT WILDFIRES
SMOKEY
SMOKEY

SMOKEY'S HOME

In 1944, the United States Forest Service created an advertising program featuring Smokey Bear to educate the public of the dangers of wildfires and how to help prevent them. Smokey's name was inspired by a New York City Fire Department hero named "Smokey" Joe Martin who suffered burns and blindness during a bold rescue in 1922.

While fighting a wildfire in the spring of 1950 that burned 17,000 acres in the Capitan Mountains of New Mexico, men rescued a badly burned black bear cub and nursed him back to health. Moved to the National Zoo in Washington, D.C., and named "Smokey," the cub became the living symbol of Smokey the Bear. The image of Smokey the Bear soon became recognized and loved nationwide as a symbol for fire prevention.

With over 17 million acres of trees, Maine is the most heavily forested state in the United States, a land where logging and lumbering is still an active way of life. The beauty of Maine's forests gives credence to its State motto of "Vacationland," drawing thousands of tourists and visitors who enjoy the great outdoor life Maine offers. In the heart of these forests lies the well-known Rangeley Lakes Region where hiking, fishing, and hunting are legendary. It is very famous for being visited by many celebrities such as movie stars and U.S. presidents, all of whom have enjoyed the best fishing and hunting in the State of Maine. The natural beauty of Maine's forestland itself is enough to always remember the symbol of Smokey the Bear as a protector from wildfires.

Camping fires, which are permitted in Maine after obtaining a permit from the Maine Forest Service, are common. They're safe if people take the proper precautions. It's important to clear away the duff down to mineral soil, to place a ring of rocks to keep the fire contained, to keep the fire small, to never leave the fire unattended, and to make sure the fire is completely out. No spark should be left behind. Remember, Smokey the Bear has his eye on you!

Within the Rangeley Lakes Region is an area referred to as the Kennebagos that consists of East Kennebago Mountain, West Kennebago Mountain, Kennebago Divide, Big Kennebago Lake, Little Kennebago Lake, and Kennebago River. I recall a time I was fishing in the Kennebagos, and I suddenly had the urge to taste a very fresh native trout cooked over an open fire. My desire was so strong I neglected Smokey's rules for safety: I did not bother to clear away duff or to place a ring of rocks around my fire. My carelessness allowed my fire to go wild, and it spread to the woods. Lucky for me I was wearing my felt "crusher" fishing hat, and I used it as a bucket to throw water on the fire and extinguish it. I had the feeling of an unknown presence around me, and I knew that Smokey the Bear was near.

Smokey's Home

I was fishing the Kennebagos
with luck that couldn't be beat.
So I stopped to build a fire
to cook a few to eat.

In my haste, I was careless.
My fire went astray.
Only with help from unknown
did I put it out that day.

When I turned around,
I saw him standing there.
Pointing straight at me was
Smokey the Fire Bear.

He said, "Help protect our forests
for all the world to see.
And remember, for all wildlife,
it's home for them and me."

Well, I learned a needed lesson.
I now use fire with care.
Every time I strike a match
I remember Smokey the Bear.

So, if you ever need a fire
during a forest roam,
please use care and remember
you're a guest in Smokey's home.

The only boot for Jeep is the boot from L.L. Bean.

A REAL NATIVE AND THE BOOT FROM L.L. BEAN

I like to boast that I am a native of Rangeley. If one should think, "What is so unusual about that?"—let me explain something. The nearest hospital to Rangeley is fifty miles down the road in a town called Farmington. In Rangeley when the mamas get ready to have their babies, the daddies put them in the car and go down to the Farmington hospital where the babies are born. A few days later the mamas and babies come back to Rangeley. Now, those babies are not natives! They were born down there in the town of Farmington, then moved to Rangeley. I'll admit, a lot of people move to Rangeley when they are only a few days old, but that does not make them a native. True Rangeley natives are quite scarce today.

The town did have a little excitement a few years back. One of the local mamas was about ready to have her baby, so the daddy helped her into the car, and they headed down the road to the Farmington hospital. Well, it seems the mama's timing was off a little bit. They didn't get very many miles down the road and the daddy had to pull the car over to the side of the road, and the baby was born right there in the car. Everything turned out fine. Daddy, mama, and baby all managed, and there were no problems.

Now the town folks all got excited. "My God! How long has it been since we had a true Rangeley native born right here in Rangeley?" they said. Everyone agreed something had to be done to document this great event. So, a group got together and drove to the spot where the baby was born to see if there was a place suitable to erect a sign saying "Birthplace of a Rangeley Native" or some other worthy quote, but they were met with grief and disappointment to discover that they were about a mile beyond the Rangeley town limits and could not lay claim to another native. "Damn!" one said. "Missed it by a mile!" Today that baby has grown into a young adult but is still known by the nickname "Almost." "Hey, how ya doing, Almost?" True Rangeley natives are hard to find these days. They just don't make them like they used to anymore. They are imported up from the town of Farmington.

Me, I was born right here in Rangeley on the old farmstead. It's the same farmstead that my father was born on. Actually, I'm a native son of a native son, and you can't get much more native than that.

You can always tell a true Rangeley native man, for he will always be wearing boots. Now, don't get the impression he has only one pair of boots. He may be wearing his woods boots, his barn boots, his church-going boots, or maybe his beer-drinking boots. But one thing is certain: if he is a true Rangeley native man, he will have boots of some kind on his feet. He wouldn't know how to walk in a pair of shoes or sneakers, and he would probably stumble or fall if he tried. All he has ever had on his feet are boots of some kind. Even as a baby he wore boots, but they were called "boot-ees."

When I think of boots, my mind wanders back to very tough times of long ago. "Born, raised, and lived dirt poor" says it all. The way of life was completely different. There were no such programs as unemployment compensation and food stamps. With skiing and snowmobiling yet to come, there were no winter tourists and only a very short, two-month summer tourist season. Winters were long, and about the only way a working man could survive was to work in the woods logging for very little pay, and at the same time, working at trying to live off the land by hunting, fishing, and gathering. When we weren't in the woods logging, we were in the woods hunting. Mostly, it was deer hunting. We didn't hunt for sport; it was done out of necessity. We needed the meat for the table. At the time, deer were plenty and game wardens were few. Plus, some of the wardens got hungry as well.

Now, whether we were in the woods logging or in the woods hunting, it was very important to have a good, sturdy pair of boots on your feet. Boots were very expensive and hard to come by, so if you had a good pair, you really appreciated it. I recall the time an old, sort of well-to-do friend of mine gave me a brand-new pair of boots, still in its original box. Never been opened. God! How excited I was! I hid that box of boots under my bed, and I thought, "I'll leave them there until I absolutely need them." And every day I walked around with a nice secure feeling knowing I had a brand-new pair of boots hidden away, safe under my bed.

I have two older brothers who I worked with in the woods. Our routine stayed pretty much the same. We would work in the woods all week; and, come Saturday, we would hang up our axes and saws, get down our rifles, and go back into the woods deer hunting to get another week's supply of meat for the table. I got up one morning and realized it was Saturday and time to get down the rifle and go hunting. I was kind of excited, for it was time to replenish our meat supply. I looked out the window and noticed that during the night it had snowed, and we had about eight inches of fresh tracking snow. My excitement grew. This could be a very successful hunting day. As I started to dress my feet, I realized my boots were completely worn out—not another mile left in them—and it was time to get out my brand-new pair of boots. Now I'm really excited. It was Saturday and time to go hunting; we had a fresh tracking snow, and I had a new pair of boots. What a great day in my life!

As I got that box of boots and opened them up, my mouth dropped open and was I ever heartbroken. They were both for the left foot! Brand-new boots, in a new box, never been worn, and there had been a mix-up in packaging. I had a pair of boots for the left foot. I noticed they were a size or two too big, but that didn't matter. It was both being for the left foot that was the disappointment. Then it hit me. I saw a lot of good coming out of this situation after all.

You see, my two older brothers had picked on me my whole life. Just because I was the youngest, they felt I was also the dumbest and couldn't do anything as well as they could. I realized here was a chance for me to get even a little bit, so I put those two left-footed boots on and wore them anyway! Now, if you want to see something funny, you want to see the tracks in the snow made by a man wearing two left boots!

What we usually did on hunting days: we would all pile into the pick-up truck before daylight and drive to a ridge that ran parallel with the road. Then one of us would get out at each end of the ridge and one at the center of the ridge; and, when it got daylight, we would hunt up the ridge, then back down. The one rule that we all had to follow was to stay in your own territory. Do not hunt outside the middle or the end of the ridge you were hunting.

Somehow, I managed to get in and out of the truck without breaking my neck, but it sure was awkward trying to steer two left boots. Since it was dark, my brothers could not see the boots on my feet, and I had them drop me off at the first end of the ridge. I had already decided to forget about hunting today; my goal was to get even with my brothers. When it got daylight and time to start up the ridge, I went very fast. When I knew I was way ahead of my brothers, I zig-zagged all over that ridge, leaving those funny two left-footed tracks everywhere. I know I must have put in ten miles or more that day just making funny tracks.

At the end of the day's hunt, we always gathered at my oldest brother's house for supper to discuss the day's hunt. I couldn't wait. I walked into the house, and one of my brothers was sitting there holding his head in his hands saying, "I don't believe it! I don't believe it!" The other brother said, "When I was in the army, I heard of a guy named Murphy who had two left feet, but I didn't think he was real!" I started to stomp my feet a little, to get their attention, so they looked down at my feet and saw I had two left boots on, and they didn't think it was funny at all. I said, "You guys just don't understand. These are very special boots. I had to send to Australia for them. They are known as 'boomerang boots' and are guaranteed to bring you back where you started from!" It's a fact, if you walk all day long with two left-footed boots on, you do have a tendency to walk in a circle a little! I've still got those boots, and I'm going to put them on someday and make those funny tracks one more time.

Now, boots are made all over the world. There are some good ones and some not so good ones. Having lived my life here in the wooded mountains of the Rangeley Lakes Region, I believe I have tried them all at one time or another. When it's time for me to buy boots, this is the way I see it:

The Boot From L.L. Bean

I've lived my life in the mountains
of these famous Rangeley Lakes
where the terrain is rough and the winters harsh
and a damn good boot it takes.

To climb the mountains, cross the creeks,
and brave the drifts of frozen snow—
like the engine does for the auto,
my feet are what make me go.

If I care for my feet, they'll care for me,
and the longer I can go without rest.
So, in buying a boot, I seek quality.
I settle for only the best.

For every year I get older,
I get a year wiser, too.
So I no longer buy the cheapest.
Only the best will do.

I want a boot that I can trust,
that's been proven for the world to see.
With years of testing and then perfection—
that's the only boot for me.

So when it's time for me to buy,
I forget the discount magazine.
The only boot for a Rangeley man
is the boot from L.L. Bean!

For about ten years, the State of Maine had an annual folk festival, The Maine Festival, and L.L. Bean was one of the major sponsors. I performed there about eight of those years; and a few days after I told that story for the first time at the Festival, I found a package in the mail from L.L. Bean. I opened it up, and there was a brand-new pair of boots.

One for the left foot, and one for the right foot!

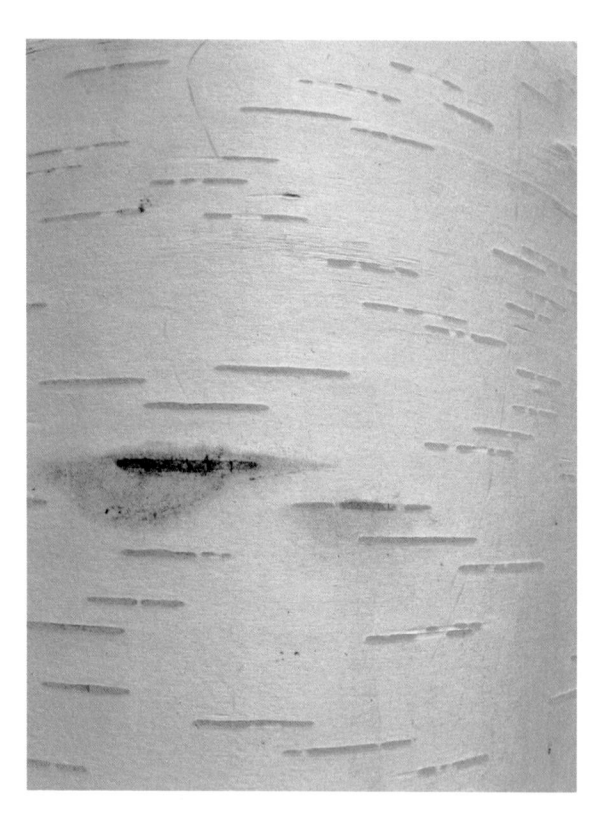

A birch tree awaiting a poem.

THE SPIRIT TREE

As a young boy wandering old logging tote roads in the big woods of the Rangeley Lakes Region, many times inspiration would hit suddenly, and I would write a poem on the white bark of a birch tree using the short stub of an indelible pencil I always had in my pocket. I'd choose a tree carefully so passersby could read the poem. I'd look for a tree close to the edge of the road, one that didn't have a branch in the way of the trunk. Then, I'd stomp all the underbrush down around the tree, and I'd start to write—always at eye level.

Often times, a few lines from a poem I read in school would cross my mind—a poem called "Trees" by a famous author named Joyce Kilmer—that begins: "I think that I shall never see / A poem lovely as a tree."

Being so young and uneducated in poetry, I couldn't make any sense out of these lines. "Kilmer is not comparing apples with apples," I thought then. "Why didn't he write, 'I think that I shall never see / A <u>flower</u> lovely as a tree.'? Why a <u>poem</u> and a tree?"

But after spending so much time among the trees in the forest, I realized that surely one of the most precious things God put on Earth is a tree, be it a tree of sweet treats such as berries, nuts, and fruit; or a tree that yields wood for the countless things we find necessary in life; or just a plain old shade tree to sit under, enjoying its beauty. A tree is symbolic of life itself.

I now see that some of the common ground a poem and a tree share is the beauty they both project, and so I understand Kilmer's poem a lot better.

Of course, the closing lines to his poem I could easily understand: "Poems are made by fools like me, / But only God can make a tree." Now, that makes sense to me! Here I am, a fool running around in the woods, leaving poems on trees!

And when I stop and think of the mighty giant redwood tree, one of the oldest living things on planet Earth—it grows from a seed so small that if I had one pound of redwood tree seeds in my hand, I would have over 250,000 seeds. For a tree that big, beautiful, and long-lasting to come from a seed so small, I believe there must be a touch of God's hand somewhere along the way.

I found it interesting to learn that Alfred Joyce Kilmer wrote several volumes of good poetry, but he is remembered, chiefly, for one single poem, and that's "Trees." Everyone should be remembered for something. And I doubt very much if I would be remembered for even one single poem, but I could be remembered in a different way.

According to mythology, the life we are assigned on Earth is doomed, but the spirit is eternal, dictating that the spirit can live on but must take a different form on Earth to do so. If that ever came to be, I want my spirit to take the form of a tree.

One time while I was hiking high on Saddleback Mountain, I came to a clearing with a huge spruce evergreen tree right on the edge. I was sitting on the ground with my back up against the tree, looking across a big valley at the faraway mountains on the other side. It came to me that just in case my spirit might take another form, I could leave it a message, hoping my spirit would see my words if it passed this way. So, I used my little jackknife and spent the entire day carving a message on the bark of the tree. And, even today, I call that spruce my Spirit Tree.

If you ever hike on Saddleback Mountain and you come across my Spirit Tree and want to read the message I left on the bark, this is pretty much what it will say:

The Spirit Tree

When my life on Earth has passed
and my spirit seeks what to be,
somehow it will know
I want to be a tree.

A worthy "King" of trees
of all the trees around,
and a tassel of cones
would be my kingly crown.

I'd be a majestic spruce tree
on a mountainside somewhere,
so I could see across the way
amidst the mountain air.

So the rain and the snow
from my trunk I could shed,
my green boughs above
like an umbrella I would spread.

My long lower branches
would be angled to the ground
to create a cozy haven
for woodland creatures around.

My heart would beat a message
carried along by winds above—
May everyone on Earth
know health, wealth, and love.

And carved upon my bark
for all passersby to see,
I would proudly wear a poem
"made by a fool like me."

And another time on Earth
again blessed I'd be,
for as a famous man once said,
"Only God can make a tree."

    Maybe Joyce Kilmer's and my spirit will cross paths sometime, somewhere. Or, who knows, maybe they already have.

Children's Day Parade.

CHILDREN'S DAY PARADE

The natural beauty of the Rangeley Lakes Region of the western Maine mountains, my homeland, is so well-known that it attracts visitors from all over, but it's still important for the town and all the local businesses to advertise. Good advertising is probably one of the most important requirements for any business to succeed, especially for us. We're not an easy day's drive for too many folks!

One of the people whose advertising did so much for the town was Elmer "Doc" Grant who owned a restaurant on Main Street. Realizing that Rangeley is located nearly on the 45th parallel of the globe, he placed a sign on his restaurant that read "Welcome to Doc Grant's Restaurant, Halfway between the Equator and the North Pole."

His sign became so popular that not only did it increase his business, it also helped draw visitors to the area just to pose in front of the sign and have their photos taken. Even after 70 years, a sign with those words on it still hangs on the original building, and people still gather for photographs.

Doc was a great promoter of the region in many other ways, too. He and his wife, Lelia, created a big event for Rangeley's Fourth of July celebration—the "Doll Carriage Parade." Little girls with their favorite dolls and carriages would parade down Main Street. This parade was enjoyed by little girls and their mothers and fathers so much that it grew into an annual event, drawing big crowds.

A few years later, realizing that little boys were left out, the Grants changed the event to the "Children's Day & Doll Carriage Parade" and invited little boys with their wagons and pets to join in. Doc handed out prizes and gifts to all the children, and he fed them ice cream from a big barrel. He ran the parade every year until he died in 1964, then other people carried on the tradition he and Lelia began.

Today, the parade is known as the "Children's Day Parade," and it is still a huge success for all—children and adults, alike. In fact, the other day I saw Peggy Lou Stevens in town for a visit. I hadn't seen her for 50 years! And I told her, "Sure, I remember you! You were the winner of Doc Grant's very first Doll Carriage Parade back in 1946!" She was some surprised.

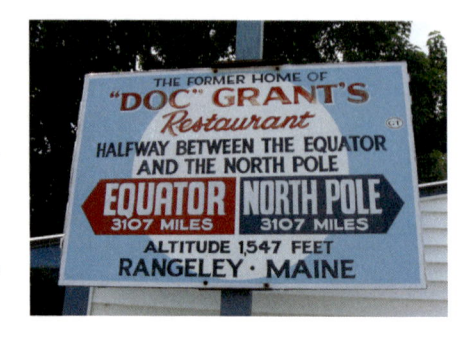

Then, back in 1981, Judy Hunger—the owner and the editor of *The Rangeley Highlander*—asked me to write a poem for the Children's Day Parade. I told her, "I don't know. It's hard to write on demand!" But then, a couple days later, it just came to me. Judy put my story-poem in the newspaper, and it's been in the *Highlander* a number of times since.

Today, when I stand on Main Street and watch the Children's Day Parade pass, I feel like I see just what Doc Grant saw many years ago. What I like, especially, is that on this day everyone in town is one, showing true community spirit.

Children's Day Parade

Following years of tradition
as summer gets underway,
once again we honor the child
as we celebrate Children's Day.

A very special day for all,
for to join a child in fun
closes all gaps in generations—
today, young and old are one.

A joy to see little toddlers
clutching their mommy's hand,
proudly showing off friends
that come from Toyland.

Baby dolls and carriages,
pets and wagons, too,
bikes, trikes, and antics
as they do what children do.

Dressed in creative costumes
with just a little help they made,
by rights each one a star—
our children on parade.

The Giving Tree.

THE GIVING TREE

Located in the western mountains of Maine, the town of Rangeley with its village of Oquossoc and its surrounding plantations make up a very close-knit community. The scenic beauty of the area that our Creator made and left up to Mother Nature to oversee is a major attraction that draws visitors from many miles away to visit, filling them with memories so powerful they return time and time again.

In addition to its country setting, a unique closeness is known by the people who dwell within its borders—a sense of community that believes in the Golden Rule of "Do unto others as you would have others do unto you," with many civic organizations and their countless volunteers who freely give so much. In fact, it would be quite appropriate if there was a sign on each end of town reading: "Entering a community of small town people with giant-sized hearts."

One such organization that is so dedicated is the Giving Tree that always gives the true spirit of Christmas, providing credence to the saying: "It's better to give than to receive." They excel at making sure everyone in need is not forgotten at Christmas time; but, most of all, they provide the community with the true spirit of giving.

The Giving Tree

Let's give a hand
to those in need,
for the joy of giving
is a joy indeed.

I urge you now,
come along with me,
and together place a gift
beneath the Giving Tree.

Give a gift for a child,
a Christmas toy for fun
where, if not for giving,
there might be none.

As we all know struggles
through these times of bad,
seeing their child have Christmas
is a gift for Mom and Dad.

Give a warm blanket
to help shut out the cold
would be a gift of comfort
for the shut-ins and old.

The true spirit of Christmas
in everyone's heart will be
the gift of "joy of giving"
from the Giving Tree.

    The balsam and resins inside of the Christmas tree combine to make a glue that gives the tree its strength and assures the needles remain attached to the tree, forever giving meaning to the word "evergreen." Without this important glue, the tree's needles would fall off like the leaves on maples and oaks; and the evergreens would be barren at Christmas time, with no greenness or fragrance.

    When we think of the Giving Tree, we see the glue that gives it strength and binds it together in the spirit of Carmen Glidden. Carmen sees with the heart, not only at Christmas time, but all year through, making her a bright light in her community, as well as on the Giving Tree.

At the Rangeley Lakes Regional School in April 2018, Tessa Sherrer taps a tree as Shirley Truland (in the background) and Beth Flynn (left) look on.

SCHOOL INSPIRATIONS: FROM TREE TO TABLE

Having been born and raised in Rangeley and having lived most of my life amidst its people and its beautiful mountain location, I am constantly surrounded by inspiration. But some of my most treasured stories are the ones that seldom get told—the stories that were inspired by students during my everyday work life as a 20-year employee of the Rangeley Lakes Regional School.

The Rangeley Lakes Regional School is a very unique school for three reasons. The first reason is that grades kindergarten through high school are all housed in the same building. A small child can enter school in his or her kindergarten year and grow and learn with the same classmates and friends for all 13 years of schooling.

The second reason is the staff. Be it teachers or secretaries, coaches or ed techs, cooks or custodians, superintendents or principals, bus drivers or substitutes, even volunteers and school board members—the word "dedication" fits all. The term "clock watching" is unknown; the term "above and beyond" is well known. I've known teachers to do whatever it takes to help students excel in everything they do. I've known teachers to give extra time—nights, weekends, and vacations—in their classrooms. I've known of out-of-pocket money some teachers have spent on unexpected necessities.

I recall the year the Senior Class asked me to be a speaker at their graduation. My theme was that the graduates of Rangeley Lakes Regional School were fortunate, for they graduated with two educations instead of one. Not only did they learn their three "Rs," they also learned how to use them, because their dedicated teaching staff took the time to teach more than what the textbook mandated. The graduates all agreed.

The third reason Rangeley Lakes Regional School is unique is the students, themselves. From generation to generation, most things change, but one thing that stays the same is that little children grow into adults. As you watch, the small elementary students play and work together; then, they enter the "just a little devilish" stage of middle school; and, finally, they go on to high school and become adults. You cannot help but notice the devotion and love and respect they show and share with each other along their 13-year journey.

I believe Rangeley Lakes Regional School is one of a kind. Now that I have explained the school's uniqueness, perhaps you can better understand why I treasure the stories that are inspired by the students so dearly.

One story that comes to mind is that for many years, each spring I observed the small elementary students and their dedicated teachers working very hard in deep snows, experiencing the actual process of collecting sap from trees and making maple syrup. Then, I realized an inspiration was taking place:

From Tree To Table

Each year, when spring comes
and winter gives up its freeze,
elementary kids and their teachers
tap the maple trees.

They drill a hole for the spile,
but the hole must be just right—
straight in, and not too big,
for the spile must fit tight.

Then they use a hammer
and tap the spile in,
quickly hang a bucket
as the drips start to begin.

Next, they gather the sap
sometime during the day,
pour it in a pan on the fire
and make it boil away.

When the sap is nearly gone
and it turns brown and thick,
they now have maple syrup,
if they take it off the fire quick.

They pour it into jars
after the syrup is cool—
yummy syrup made by small ones
at Rangeley Lakes Regional School.

Bruce Collins.

SCHOOL INSPIRATIONS: A MOMENT'S WORTH

If I recall correctly, it was in 1984 when an incident happened with a student that inspired a story; and that story came to me so fast, it took me longer to write it down than it did to create it. My custodial job had always been a busy one, and many times several things happened at the same time. Sometimes it was very frustrating not being able to finish one job before being interrupted to start on another. The school building is sprawled out, it lies low to the ground, and its roof is flat. So, on a daily basis, countless balls were kicked or thrown up on the roof, and they'd get trapped. Then, I had to climb up through a hatch to retrieve them. It was a very small job that I didn't mind doing until I realized that I was going up on the roof three and four times a day!

These interruptions from other work had gotten out of hand, and I thought a change was needed. I met with the principal and the teachers, and all agreed to a new rule: I would go up once a week and get all the balls. The important thing was to make sure that the kids understood this so they would be more careful. This was done, and everyone knew not to even ask me to go up on the roof.

The very next day, I was struggling with a very uncooperative tractor with a fouled plug that had also fouled my mood, when the voice of a young third-grade boy pleaded, "Jeep, please get my ball for me?" I didn't explode, but I did firmly tell the boy that I was busy, and that he knew the rule. He didn't say any more; but, as he turned and walked away, I will never forget the look on his face and in his eyes. I wasn't as tough as I thought I was, and I told him to wait a minute while I went up on the roof and got his ball.

As I placed the ball in his hand, I hardly heard his "Thanks, Jeep." The new look of happiness in his eyes and on his face was overwhelming. The inspiration was so strong, like I said, it took longer to write the story-poem down than it did to create it in my mind. I called the story—

A Moment's Worth

During my busy day,
as endless tasks do mount,
I hurry and I scurry
to make my moments count.

For in summing up the jobs
I have not done yet,
seems the hurrier I go,
the behinder I get.

When a voice pierced my thoughts,
I glanced up to see
a small child who said,
"Please get my ball for me."

"I'm very busy, kid," said I,
"I have many things to do.
Your ball will have to wait.
I have no time for you."

Then as I saw the sadness
in the eyes of one so small,
I realized a tree without branches
is like a child without its ball.

So, as I spared a moment
for this added chore,
I learned a value of time
I had not known before.

> And as my weary day ended,
> I thought back and smiled.
> Today I used a precious moment
> to look through the eyes of a child.

The young boy who inspired "A Moment's Worth" was Bruce Collins. Bruce graduated in 1994, in that class that dedicated the yearbook to "Special People In Our Lives." Just a few short years after graduating, Bruce passed away. To be called home to Heaven at such a young age is sad indeed. I'll always be indebted to Bruce for inspiring me to stop and look at things from a child's point of view. It helped make me a better person.

Bruce's family asked me to read the poem at Bruce's funeral service, but I knew that I would not be able to handle it. So, Jerome "Frenchie" Guevremont read it, and he said that he just barely got through it. Every time I think back and recall the look in Bruce's eyes that allowed me to understand his need, a famous quote by Antoine de Saint Exupéry from his story *The Little Prince* comes to mind, for I believe it helped me on that day: "It is only with the heart that one can see rightly; what is essential is invisible to the eye." Over the years, I feel I have become accustomed to seeing with the heart.

Rangeley Lakes Regional School.

SCHOOL INSPIRATIONS: SPECIAL PEOPLE IN OUR LIVES

Rangeley Lakes Regional School is unique for several reasons, but the most important reason is that 13 grades of students, from kindergarten through high school, are all housed in the same building. A small child can enter school in his or her kindergarten year, and grow and learn with all the same friends for all 13 years of schooling. So, that results in a closeness that's just like family. Growing up in a small, close-knit community, children also spend their out-of-school time together, which adds strength to the ties that bind. The closeness makes fond memories of happy school days but teary-eyed graduations, for it's like a family's parting of the ways when they go on to begin their adult lives.

I recall my 13th year of employment, because that year I saw my first kindergarten class graduate from high school. As I stood in the gym during graduation, I thanked each graduate with all my heart for allowing me to be a part of their lives for 13 years. The graduates wanted to recognize the support the community had given them throughout their school days, and they asked me to write a story-poem that would enable them to thank the special people in their lives. They dedicated their yearbook to these special people, and the students felt that the words of my poem said exactly what they wanted to say:

Special People In Our Lives

We enter this world so helpless,
needing constant care.
And as we grow and learn,
we find guidance everywhere.

We find it in Grandpa's tales
of the good ole days they had.
We are guided by Mom and Dad
through times both good and bad.

And all through our school days
our need for guidance never ends.
We find it with our teachers,
our neighbors, peers, and friends.

We find it in our community—
everyone seems to understand,
like the Rotary, Boosters, and RFA.
They guide us with a helping hand.

So now we take a moment,
as our graduation day arrives,
and bless the times we've been touched
by the "Special People In Our Lives."

Jeep Wilcox speaks to the graduates at the 1990 Rangeley Lakes Regional School Graduation Ceremony. From left to right: Bobby Haley, Nate Bean, Jeep Wilcox, Serena Belanger, and Larry Allen.

SCHOOL INSPIRATIONS:
I SEE

An unforgettable time in young people's lives is their high school graduation. A lot of extra time and expense goes into preparing for this cherished event. One of the highlights that Rangeley School graduates always take pride in is their selection of guest speakers for the Commencement Exercise. Over the years, they have invited U.S. Senators, people who hold Ph.Ds and other professional degrees, and many motivational speakers. Having been a school employee in the maintenance department for 22 years, I was very honored, of course, to have been selected as guest speaker in 1990 and again in 2004.

In 1990, the theme for my address was praise for this small school's ability to provide individualized attention to students, as well as praise for the community that provided a supportive atmosphere for young people. Unknown to me at the time, that same praise was exactly the theme that the class valedictorian, Roberta Haley, had chosen, so our companion speeches brought a feeling of closeness to everyone.

The year 2004 was a little different. It was a year of tight budgets and differences in politics that resulted in cuts in school programs that saddened many students as well as many members of the community. As a result, many of the graduates felt that they were not as appreciated as they should have been. So, I based my 2004 speech on the theme of all the possibilities the future held for this graduating class, to show them that they were one of best and most intelligent classes ever. As I stood on the stage with the graduates, I addressed a packed-full, standing-room-only gymnasium and recited this poem:

I See

To Rangeley Lakes Regional School's Graduation Class of 2004

As I stand here today
with Rangeley's graduates with me,
I cast a look into the future
to see what I can see.

I see an artist, a scientist,
I see an attorney at law.
I see the skilled hand of a surgeon,
being the best I ever saw.

I see a member of the armed forces,
being all they can be,
proudly serving above and beyond
to help keep our country free.

I see a movie star, a great musician.
Definitely, I see a teacher or two.
I can see an elite member
of NASA's astronaut crew.

I see an architect, an engineer.
I see the winner of an Olympic event.
I see a senator, a congressman,
maybe even a President.

I see all these things possible,
plus potential for so much more
when I see Rangeley's graduates
of the year two thousand four.

So congratulations, Graduates,
on your very special day.
The world anxiously awaits you.
May the best come your way.

Rodney Richard, Sr., carves a bear at his home, Main Street, Rangeley.

THE MAD WHITTLER

Before today's recycling at modern transfer facilities, most rural Maine towns had open dumps for the disposal of garbage and all other unwanted items. Everything was just thrown into a pile. When the pile got too high, it was leveled with a bulldozer; and, from time to time, it was burned. But—it was not buried or covered over until it was permanently closed.

Believe it or not, these town dumps were an improvement because at one time out here in the country everybody would have their own dump right at their home. Even some businesses had their own dumps. And the only cover they had was natural leaves and bushes that grew up over them. But finally, the towns got organized enough, started cleaning up the countryside, and having their own dumps.

But—these town dumps were pretty unsightly, so to hide them from view as much as possible, the towns put them in out-of-the-way places, on the edge of the forest. And, of course, these dumps attracted animals, like bears.

Compared to other towns, my hometown of Rangeley had an abundance of food waste. You stop and think about all the hotels during the hotel era—places like the Rangeley Lake Hotel, Mingo Springs Hotel, The Barker, Mountain View Hotel, York's Loon Lake Log Village—they had a big supply of food waste, and most of it went on the open dump, too.

So, the town dump served two purposes: it was a collection point for people's garbage so it wasn't strewn all over the countryside, and it was a forage point for the bears. And in Rangeley, the dump's new location was ideal for both. In 1972, the dump was moved from the end of Robbins Avenue to a site out of town, halfway to Oquossoc, on the left, across from Quimby Pond Road.

The dump was on a slight hill that had a heavily evergreen-forested valley below. Since it was surrounded by trees, the bears had quick access to cover. They'd leave the dump, cross the wooded valley, and then go up along a ridge where they lived. They traveled back and forth each night; and, sometimes, they even came during the day. But mostly, they came once it got dark.

And of course, the word spread about the bears, and people started driving from all around to see them foraging on the dump. The first eight or ten cars to arrive would line up with their headlights on, to light up the whole dump. This turned into quite a crowd-drawing event. There were times when both sides of the road would be lined with cars. And, from May until September, it was happening all the time.

It got as big as smelting, and smelting was once one of the biggest things in Rangeley. People came from miles around to go smelting for two to three weeks as the coves and brooks opened up, usually in April, on the Kennebago River at Route 16. Cars would be lined up for a mile and a half on each side of the road. Hundreds of cars! Everybody was down to the river, smelting! It got so big that the Rotary built a lunch wagon and went out on site, on Friday and Saturday nights, just for the smelters. Of course, there's no smelting anymore there, but the bear-watching crowd got to be that big, or bigger.

I can't imagine the money that came into Rangeley from the bears. Usually there were two big nights—Friday and Saturday. And if people stayed the whole weekend, of course they had to stay in a hotel, they had to have food, they had to have gas—all because they wanted to watch the bears on the dump.

But—all things in nature come in cycles: fruit, berries, wildlife. There's a bumper crop, then it thins out to almost nothing. Up and down, up and down. And in this particular case, it truly happened. The bears got scarce. It wasn't over-hunting; it was just nature's cycle. People who used to see 12 or 14 bears all in one night were lucky to see one or two bears. It got so bad that the State started talking about shutting down bear hunting season.

You can imagine what happened. The Chamber of Commerce, the guides and sportsmen—everyone was concerned, because without the bears, they would have a much smaller tourist crowd in town. So, they had a meeting in the Legion Hall to discuss the situation.

Now, when small towns have meetings, they often hold them at the school or the town office; but in Rangeley at that time, most of the town meetings were at the American Legion Hall. This was long before the big new Rangeley School or the Guides and Sportsmen's Hall in Oquossoc. The Legion Hall was usable and accessible; it was right on Main Street, by the lake. People played beano at the Legion on Saturday nights, and my uncle Sam Dunham ran beano every week for pretty near 30 years. The Legion Hall was a focal point for Rangeley.

So, during this time when bears were scarce, I happened to see Rodney Richard, Rangeley's Mad Whittler (1929-2015), carving his wooden bears with his chain saw; and I came up with an idea about how to provide a solution for the problem:

The Mad Whittler

The Legion Hall was full
that night in town—
a discussion on bears,
the population was down.

Business folk from town
and the Chamber of Commerce
all agreed the situation
couldn't be worse.

For to watch the bears
was a crowd-drawing event
where a lot of tourist dollars
each year were spent.

Sportsmen and guides,
they were concerned too,
for without lots of bears,
what would they do?

When up spoke Rodney,
being slightly amused:
"To attract something,
a good decoy is used.

"Now you folks don't worry,
I have a plan
that will bring back the bears,
if anything can."

He whittled many a night,
he whittled many a day,
he whittled Saddleback Mountain
nearly all away.

When he finished,
the results were good—
one life-looking decoy
where every tree had stood.

And one month later
as the sun was going down,
bears were still coming
from miles around.

Three cheers for Rodney!
He deserves a hand
for bringing back the bears
all over our land.

We should whittle out a Rodney
and erect it in a park,
surround it by lights,
so it can be seen in the dark.

At his feet
we should place this sign—
"Rodney, the Mad Whittler,
A Legend in His Time."

Rodney Richard, Sr., carves a bear at his home, Main Street, Rangeley.

ARE FAIRY TALES REAL?

I've always felt kind of fortunate. I was born and raised here in Rangeley, a small community where everybody knows everybody—or, at least we used to! And growing up, you knew who lived on this side of the street, you knew who lived on that side of the street, and you knew who lived 20 miles down the road. You knew the names of all the mamas and daddies in the neighborhood, you knew the names of all the kids. You even knew the names of all the cats and dogs in the neighborhood. It was a real close-knit community.

When my brothers and sisters and I got bored, we used to take the Rumford phone directory and go to the Rangeley section. And the game we used to play—I was 11 or 12—we'd go line by line, starting with the As, Bs, and Cs, all the way to the Ws, Ys, and Zs. And it was very, very rare we didn't know a person and exactly where they lived. Everybody knew everybody. Everybody gave everybody a helping hand. It was really a joy growing up like that.

And I grew up with another fellow in Rangeley, a very interesting man. I'm sure a lot of you have heard about him. His name is Rodney Richard, he's known as The Mad Whittler. Now Rodney was a very, very talented man. He went all over the countryside and he went to Russia, too. He was so fascinating a carver because he could carve or whittle anything you could imagine, using any kind of tool you could imagine. It just came to him. It was a really, really nice gift.

What made him so famous were the chain saw carvings he did of Maine's black bears. Now, a chain saw is a good tool if you want to go into the woods and do some logging or if you want to saw up some firewood, but to carve something, to shape something, boy, it's a pretty rough tool! And it's a pretty hard thing to do. Rodney spent his entire life in the woods, using a chain saw and doing some logging, so he could do anything with it.

There was a time when I couldn't resist leaving a little poem on a tree—and Rodney couldn't resist acting up with his chain saw. So, a truck load of logs would arrive down at the mill, and one of the logs sticking off the end of the truck would be shaped like a bear's head. Right away, they knew where those logs came from: Rodney up there in Rangeley, fooling around with his chain saw.

Everywhere I go, I take one of Rodney's bears, so people can get a better look at what I'm talking about. Rodney called him "Jeep's Traveling Bear." This bear has really been some places with me. It's been to Vermont, it's been to Delaware, it's been to Massachusetts. It's been clean out to Seattle, Washington. And it didn't have to ride in the baggage! It rode right up front with me.

Rodney did an excellent job, but what really fascinates me about Rodney is that he carved these bears in all sizes, from as small as my fist to 10 feet tall. He made them looking to the left, looking to the right, standing on their hind legs, walking on all fours. It didn't matter to Rodney, it was all the same to him.

When he got all done with a bear, he'd roll it over on its back and put his mark on the bear's paw. How he did it depended on the size, whether it was a big bear or a little bear. If it was a big bear, he'd carve his initials on the bear's paw with a knife. If it was a little bear, he'd stamp its paw: "Rodney Richard, The Mad Whittler." That was his trademark. Then Rodney'd get a bucket of black stain and give it a coat of black. No matter where you are in the United States, you see a bear similar to this wood-carved bear of mine, go up and check its paw. If you see "Rodney, The Mad Whittler" on there, you know that bear came from Rangeley, Maine.

Rodney did a very good job. His bears look pretty real. Lifelike. I got three or four bears of Rodney's at home on the lawn, and I got them positioned underneath the pine tree, back from the road. And all the time, there's cars stopping out front. They think there's some real bears out there.

One thing that Rodney has done for me more than anything: he restored my belief in fairy tales. I'll see if I can explain what I mean:

Are Fairy Tales Real?

As a boy I read a story
of a man who wanted a son.
So out of a block of wood,
he carved and whittled one.

Then along came the fairy
with her magic wand,
and out of a wooden puppet,
Pinocchio was born.

You say this could not happen.
It just could not be.
But before you judge too quickly,
hear what happened to me.

I was up on Saddleback Mountain,
a bear cub I did spy.
He was trapped between two boulders,
and I could hear his mournful cry.

Feeling some added strength
develop inside of me,
I separated those boulders.
That little bear jumped free.

In his eyes I could see the gratitude.
He was not afraid of man.
He showed it in the way
he gently licked my hand.

But as he turned to go,
I could not believe what I saw—
"Rodney, The Mad Whittler"
was stamped there on his paw.

"Dancing Bears," carved by Rodney Richard, Sr.

BROTHER OF THE BEAR

For 30 years or more, my custodial job at the Rangeley Lakes Regional School took me traveling down Main Street every day to get the mail. So, I'd always be going right by Rodney and Lucille Richard's house, and many times Rodney would be out there by his "Mad Whittler" shop, bent over and running the chain saw. Quite often, I would pull into the driveway and watch him for five or ten minutes. And, because of the noise of the chain saw, he wouldn't even know I was around. Sometimes, I'd sneak up and take a picture.

I am so fascinated by his work—all of his carvings—but, especially, his bears because they look so real. Take the way their heads are pointed: some of them might be looking down, some might be looking up. His dancing bears, the way he's shaped their arms around each other—it looks like they're hugging. And his standing bears, you put one off on the edge of a field, and it looks like a real one, just waiting, sniffing the air.

Then, one time, I caught Rodney taking a break, and we started talking about his carving. "How can you possibly take a rough tool like a chain saw," I asked him, "and make something that looks so real?!" And he told me, "Anything I can see in my mind, I can carve. So, if my bears look real, it comes from a memory, in my mind. But, basically, it's all done by feel."

I didn't say it to him at the time, but, to me, his bears look too real to have been done just by feel. There's something more powerful involved, and I've been trying to figure it out.

No matter what size bear he was carving, you would think the first thing he'd have to do was find the right-sized log and make some measurements. I've seen some sculptors work, and they keep checking with a tape measure to keep on track: "How far should it be from his ear down to his shoulder? How far across his belly?" But that never happens with Rodney. He got what he judged to be the right-sized log and made his carvings adjust to that. He didn't make any marks on the log. If he started with the bear's head first, how could he be so certain that the belly was going to be in the right place, and the feet were going to be in the right place, and that he wasn't going to run out of wood and have start all over again? But he never ran out of wood, and he never made a mistake.

And when you were standing there watching him—the sawdust was flying, he was rolling the bear over and over again, and he was taking a little off here and a little off there—you were watching it all come to shape, but you could hardly believe it. How could his bears come to shape and never fail?

A lot of artists use a pattern or a template—something to go by—but Rodney didn't. He just took a log and away he went. The ears on his bears were always in the right place; the paws were always in the right place; and, no matter whether the bear's got one ear cocked or whether he's holding one paw out, everything fell in the right place. How could Rodney do this? How could he do this without a plan, without a pattern, without a guide?

Sure, his knowledge of chain saws and bears came from a lifetime of logging in the Maine woods, but where did he get the ability to make his bears look so real? How many real bears had Rodney held in his arms? How many bears had he seen in zoos? How many bears had he sculpted in art school? None!! It all came so easy to him. He just took a saw and made it happen. I'm not saying he didn't get aching muscles. And I know his bears are made out of wood, but how did he make them look like so much more than a whittled piece of wood, like they were not made out of wood at all? There's something else.

So, later, while I was sitting there in my truck watching Rodney carve another bear, I remembered what he told me about doing it all by feel, and I thought to myself, "Ah, no, no, no, Rodney. That's just your modest way of talking. It's more than that! You're seeing something else that nobody beside you can see." And then it came to me, and I realized what that something else might be:

Brother Of The Bear

As I sit and watch him carving,
he says it's done by feel,
but the results are amazing—
Rodney's bears look so real.

So I sensed he had a secret
he cared not to share,
a secret one night I learned—
he's a Brother of the Bear.

I followed him up Saddleback Mountain
in the late hours of the night.
Every star was twinkling,
the moon was shining bright.

He came upon a clearing,
yelled a sound not heard before,
and out of the woods a-running
came forty bears or more.

As the bears gathered around him,
somehow they seemed to say,
"Welcome home, our brother.
Stop awhile, and play."

Well, they wrestled and they frolicked.
For hours they had fun.
Like a scene from *Grizzly Adams*,
man and beast were one.

Now, of course, we all know
that bears do not cry,
but the moment Rodney left,
there was a tear in every eye.

Now as I watch him carving
from where I'm sitting there,
in my heart I know his secret—
he's a Brother of the Bear.

Rangeley Lakes, Maine, Promenade at The Rangeley Lake House.

WALKS OF LIFE

As I was growing up, I often recalled an adage my grandparents would sometimes quote, "To see how small you really are, go stand by the ocean." Being raised in Maine's western mountains, I always thought it would have been better said: "To see how small you really are, go climb a mountain."

Believe me, if you stand at the summit of Saddleback Mountain, turn in a 360-degree circle, and see majestic mountains on every point of the compass as far as the eye can see, you feel very small. As you view your surroundings, you become humbled by the power of our Creator. Not only can you feel and see the beauty that surrounds you—the icing on the cake is the constant smell of balsam that permeates body and soul. A mountain range many miles long, known as the Longfellow Mountains, with peaks so high you look down, not up, to watch the eagles soar, fills you with a sense of being attuned with the forces of nature. What a joy it would be to shed all burdens and spend life wandering Maine's High Peaks. Truly the "higher" the Maine peak you walk on is a walk nearer to Heaven itself.

Walks Of Life

Some walk down the aisle,
joined hand in hand,
to start a life together,
bound by a golden band.

Some walk through the garden
in the early dawn hours,
while refreshing dew
clings to awakening flowers.

Some walk through the park,
watching little children play.
Some walk during sunset,
at the closing of the day.

Some walk along the seashore
on grains of sand so fine.
Some walk beside babbling brooks,
enjoying peace of mind.

Some walk the straight and narrow,
like the Good Book says we should.
Some walk down memory lane,
recalling times of childhood.

But in all walks of life,
can one be more divine
than a walk among "Maine's High Peaks"
with soul soothed by balm of pine?

Harland Wilcox.

THE MISSING ONE

Born and raised the seventh child in a family of 12 on a hardscrabble farm, money was scarce, but happiness was plentiful. Love and concern among siblings in a large family seemed to add strength to the family values. One member's hurt is everyone's hurt. Devotion and concern were shared equally, but 12 births spanning 24 years didn't necessarily mean everyone shared the same interests at the same time in their lives. The interests of a 16-year-old differed from a six-year-old's. The closeness in age seemed to strengthen the ties that bind.

One of my brothers—Harland—being only two years older than I, while growing up, we became inseparable. Whether doing our chores or hunting and fishing, our ways became one. It was often said we were so close, it reminded people of the well-known picture of a boy from Father Flanagan's Boys Town, carrying another on his back with the caption: "He ain't heavy Father . . . he's m' brother."

Teenage years pass swiftly; and, while I was 15, my brother turned 17 and proudly enlisted in the U.S. Army to serve his country, which I also did when I turned 17. The two years I had to wait to follow him were long and lonely and also became the saddest.

In November of 1950, my brother was one of 2,500 U.S. Army soldiers engaged in combat with enemy troops on the east side of the Chosin Reservoir in North Korea. Those U.S. Army troops, thinking the battle would be short and they would be home for Christmas, were taken by surprise when, on November 27th, 20,000 Chinese troops that had unknowingly massed, surrounded them with relentless onslaught, including hand-to-hand combat. Those U.S. Army troops were outnumbered eight to one.

The battle's lasting four days and five nights certainly speaks of the bravery and determination of our troops. By the time the order came on December 1st to withdraw to Hagaru-ri at the southern tip of the Reservoir, the U.S. troops were reeling with heavy casualties—many killed, wounded, or taken prisoner.

I vividly recall December 12th, 1950, thirteen days before Christmas, as the messenger from Western Union delivered the telegram from the Department of the Army: "With regret, missing in action." Three years later, in 1953, my brother was reported "assumed dead but unaccounted for." The Department of the Army has family blood on file for DNA testing, in case any remains are found. But with the passing of nearly 70 years, hope is fading that the military's most sacred vow—"Until they are home"—will be fulfilled, bringing closure for both the Department of the Army and myself.

In the center of my hometown of Rangeley, there is a granite war memorial inscribed with names of those from the Rangeley Lakes Region who answered our country's call and served in the Armed Forces, including the names of my father and his five sons. It's a very impressive list of names from a community so small, and it gives me a deep feeling of being hometown proud. It also provides me with some consolation. Each Memorial and Veterans Day as I visit the gravesites of family and friends who have passed on—there being no site for my missing brother—I view the war memorial as a substitute, clinging to hope that his remains will be found and returned to his homeland, no longer to be the missing one.

The Missing One

"Missing in action,"
the telegram said.
"With regret, we can't say
if he is alive or dead."

Though half a century has passed,
the roll-call is the same:
"Unaccounted for" is answered
when they call his name.

But did he die fighting
for his country that day?
Or was he taken prisoner
and carried far away?

Does he lie in a dungeon
walled by cold stone,
believing he is forgotten
by those at home?

Is he a victim of brainwash,
now a disoriented man,
living a strange life
in a foreign land?

Does the search go on
across the battleground,
seeking his remains that
have never been found?

Yes, my heart still carries
an ache of sorrow and woe,
but the unbearable pain
is the "never to know."

I see no medals
pinned to his chest.
I see no remains
laid to final rest.

No yellow ribbons
wrapped around a tree.
Nowhere a symbol
of hope I can see.

So, aimlessly I wander
each Memorial Day,
with no graveside to visit
or to kneel at and pray.

The only hope I carry
to ease the burden I bear:
being unaccounted for could mean
he still serves somewhere.

But until the time comes
his remains are found,
a memorial to those who served
is my hallowed ground.

At Height of Land, overlooking Mooselookmeguntic Lake.

BEAUTY ALL AROUND

Most of us are familiar with the saying "One picture is worth a thousand words." It carries a lot of truth, but there are times when a very clear picture isn't complete without some words to go with it. A good example would be sitting up all night on Christmas Eve trying to put a child's toy together, or going to a department store and buying something that has to be assembled. The carton has a picture of what it looks like, but where would we be without the assembly instructions that come with it? The picture is good, the words are good, but joining them both together makes it very complete.

One of my best-known stories is the first one I joined with a picture, and it's a story that came to me very fast. I was visiting a very special spot that I used to visit a lot when I was a young boy, known as Height of Land. The view is so breathtaking, visitors come from far away to see it. It's my belief that very few visitors have seen it only once, for after seeing it for the first time, they just have to return and see it again. You can see the view from a mountainside overlooking Mooselookmeguntic Lake, about 12 miles down mountain from the village of Oquossoc in the Rangeley Lakes Region.

As I was sitting on the ground enjoying the beauty of the view, it came to me that it looked exactly the way it did when I was a small boy. In fact, I believed it must have looked the same as it did when just the native Indians lived here and gave the waters the name of Mooselookmeguntic. When that thought hit me, the words started coming to mind so fast. I had no scrap paper to write on, but I didn't want to lose my concentration. Then, I spied a piece of bark fallen from a white birch tree lying beside the road. I managed to write the whole story just as it came to me;

but, since the surface of the bark was so irregular and my writing was so fast, it took a little time for me to read it afterward. Quite appropriately, the story applied its own title: "Beauty All Around."

I shared this story with an audience at The Maine Festival one time; and on the long drive home, I realized how much they enjoyed the story. I felt it was a shame, though, that they couldn't see what the inspiration for the story was; so, I took a photo of the scene and had a graphic house put it and my words together, creating a marriage of story and inspiration. This composition has been very successful; hundreds of visitors from as many as 44 states in the United States, as well as five foreign countries, have taken copies home. It's been presented to two U. S. senators, two of State of Maine governors, as well as three movie stars who have visited Rangeley.

Let me share this beautiful spot with you:

Beauty All Around

Indian legends tell us
they had a chanting sound.
Sacred to them, it means
there's "Beauty all around."

But that was years ago,
when they had their way,
and the beauty they had found
was long before my day.

For in our modern times,
I really must confess,
it's hard to find much beauty
in the way we must progress.

We need our high-rise buildings
so life can keep its pace,
and, for future progress,
we're exploring outer space.

Our industries are a must,
though most of them pollute.
We can't close our coal mines,
and then, of course, there's nukes.

We live with an arms race.
Should someone get rude,
that will see us all in Hell,
fighting for bubbling crude.

But there's a place I know
in the mountains of Maine
where legends still are heard.
Things are pretty much the same.

If you ever get to go there,
listen for their sound.
The echoes are still ringing—
there's "Beauty all around."

SEEING IS BELIEVING

So many things we hear about today that are thought to exist but are hard to believe bring to mind the old saying: "Seeing is believing." Your mind can create an image of what something is supposed to look like, but it actually needs to be seen with the eye to decide if you believe it exists or not. A couple of examples would be Nessy, the Loch Ness monster; or Bigfoot, the Abominable Snowman; and, of course, UFOs.

It may be easier to decide about Nessy or Bigfoot, for it is narrowed down to thinking of a creature that could be part human and part animal being on Earth to begin with. With a UFO, it is quite different.

To see a brilliant light in the distant sky moving erratically, we first have to decide if it could be a man-made object like a plane, a rocket, or perhaps a weather balloon—or, if it could be an act of nature, like an asteroid or a falling star. Only then could we decide if it could be extraterrestrial visitors from afar.

If it's believed to be aliens visiting planet Earth from outer space, then we must wonder from where and how. To believe or not to believe?

In deciding, we must give thought to so much advancement in modern technology in so little time. Since 1903 in Kitty Hawk, North Carolina, where Orville and Wilbur Wright made the first controlled and sustained airplane flight in history, only 115 years have passed. In that time, we've seen many amazing fighter planes in several wars and, advancing to the present day, jet fighters and helicopters. Huge jet airliners capable of carrying hundreds of passengers many thousands of miles non-stop now appear all over the world. Man has flown to the moon, landed, walked on its surface, and returned safely. Man has put two dune buggies on planet Mars with plans to send a human there soon.

It tells us that it's not inconceivable to believe UFOs could be hovering in front of us less than a thousand feet away, and it certainly gives credence to "Seeing is believing."

Seeing Is Believing

They say, "Seeing is believing,
believe only what you see,"
and what I saw one evening
made a believer out of me.

I was fishing on Saddleback Mountain,
from the shore of a remote pond.
I was after a trout for my supper.
It wouldn't take me long.

Just as I hooked a big one,
fire lighted up the sky,
and a UFO was descending.
I let out a startled cry.

Like something out of *Star Trek*,
its strange windows I could see,
and the weird sound it was making
sure made a believer out of me.

In those windows I could see shadows.
Somebody was there, inside.
So I uttered a little prayer,
"Please! Don't take me for a ride!"

Straight down it came diving.
Then, it started rocking to and fro.
And like a piece of charcoal burning,
suddenly it started to glow!

I threw away my fish-pole.
Down that mountainside I run.
'Cause fishing with those aliens
ain't my idea of fun!

So, listen you unbelievers,
this story I tell is true.
Had you seen what I saw,
it would make a believer out of you.

A Logger's Memorial. On February 21, 1996, forty-eight-year-old Melvin Theriault of Ashland, Maine, met death when his logging truck— a Ford LTL 9000—left the road and slipped sideways into the snowy woods.

DEER MOUNTAIN RUN

Be it in present times or days gone by, our country's unsung heroes definitely include the drivers of the "big rigs" in the trucking industry who keep our nation on the move. Although modern technology has made trucks larger, safer, and more powerful—so, more cost effective by allowing the moving of heavier payloads, many of our nation's highways have not kept up with the demand for improvements; so drivers, to compensate, have been required to gain experience in self-taught skills.

From coast to coast, many sections of highways have become known for their dangers due to truckers talking shop at truckstops or being highlighted in songs inspired by those dangers—songs that mention Wolf Creek Pass in the San Juan Mountains of Colorado or Feather River Canyon in Plumas County of California, and the well-known song about the Haynesville Woods in Maine, which has a line: "If they'd buried all the truckers lost in them woods, there'd be a tombstone every mile."

Maine's western mountains have very little flat land. Truckers say you are driving uphill or downhill with curves so sharp you blow your horn at your own taillight. The lengths of the grades are measured in miles, not yards. The region's wicked "three-mile grade" is actually nearer five miles long and very winding, leaving no room for error.

Entering the town of Phillips, Blake and Walker Hill is over a mile long, with a sharp curve at the bottom. A runaway bridge was built across Sandy River to an intervale to allow truckers to escape in case of burned out brakes or misjudgment in bailing gears that would end in free-wheeling.

Saddleback Mountain is so steep that a logging road down one of its sides had to be built in a zig-zag pattern, requiring five miles of construction to travel one mile down mountain. Even with some modern highway improvements, it's hard to judge whether it's for the better—like the recent construction to bypass Horseshoe Corner at Small's Falls by creating a 10% grade that has become known locally to many as Suicide Hill.

Just because a mountain is high doesn't necessarily mean it has the worst roads crossing it. Deer Mountain, only 3,500 feet in elevation, is a mountain of granite boulders and rock outcroppings, and the roads follow a footprint of Native American trails that cross the mountains between the States of Maine and New Hampshire. Being located along the 45th parallel, the mountain lies in a snowbelt where many times the sun is shining on each side of the mountain while snow is falling heavily on the summit. Quite often, it will snow and freeze unexpectedly in July and August, making driving so unpredictable even the Devil says a prayer when passing by. A trucker driving only one time over Deer Mountain meets the criteria for entrance into the Truckers Hall of Fame.

Deer Mountain Run

Truckers fear those "Haynesville Woods"
where driving "big rigs" can be a trial,
alert to the constant dangers
by seeing "tombstones every mile."

Truckers curse "Wolf Creek Pass"
with countless hazards galore,
or when they face the Devil
driving "Feather River Canyon" floor.

But a trucking tale of horror
that makes others seem like fun
are tales born in Rangeley, Maine,
driving the Deer Mountain run.

Hairpin curves like ribbon candy,
no room for any mistake.
When engineers mapped this highway,
for a pattern they used a snake.

The road over the top is long.
Truck bumpers scrape the sky.
Slipping and sliding on ice and snow
in the middle of July.

But when they reach the summit,
if weather is clear and fair,
they can "breaker-one" to Heaven
and talk to angels there.

A tribute to all brave truckers
from near or from afar—
if you've driven over Deer Mountain,
you've looked down on a star.

As truckers keep on trucking,
they age each year by one.
But each year they age twenty
driving that Deer Mountain run.

When truckers' work on Earth is done,
in Heaven forever they will dwell.
If they trucked over Deer Mountain,
they have already been to Hell.

Rangeley Lake.

THE EIGHTH DAY

The woods of the Rangeley Lakes Region in Maine are vast indeed. Stand anywhere and look around you, and you will see deep woods for miles and miles. I think back to how young I was when I first started wandering off into the woods; and, by today's standards, it's very scary. When I was five and six, my parents could not leave me outside unattended, for I would wander off into the woods. By the time I was 10, the woods were like a big magnet, drawing me deeper and deeper into them. The meaning of the word fear was totally unknown to me. Deep inside I felt I was meant to be a part of the valleys, streams, wildlife, and mountains; and the biggest attraction was the trees. It was like home, and I definitely belonged. To this very day, while I say that it's in my blood, my wife says that it's because I'm not very far removed from an animal in my life. I guess we are both saying the same thing.

During my young school days, I used to skip school a lot and go wandering up into the tree-covered mountains. Needless to say, I was in trouble a lot with both my teachers and my parents, but the pull was so strong, I could not resist.

Trying to do the right thing, my parents also made me attend Sunday school so I would grow up learning about God and His work, as well as the three "Rs" of regular school. Again the woods would win out, and I would skip Sunday School and go climb a mountain. So, of course, I didn't learn what the other kids learned about God's work and ways.

Later on in my life, I found myself at a happy, special occasion down country in the State of Delaware, involved in a conversation with a man of the cloth. Not only did I find him a very nice man as a person, but also a man who was very good at his profession and who was an excellent representative of God's works and ways. Now as I have pointed out, my learnings of God's works are not as plentiful as most folks', and talking with an expert, I would be better off keeping my mouth shut and listening. He asked me, "Do you go to church on Sundays?"

Now we all know that lying is a sin, and I wasn't about to lie to one of God's reps, so I replied, "Hardly ever." For the next half hour or so his words were quite powerful, explaining how I should remember the Sabbath to keep it holy, go to a place of worship of my choosing, and concentrate on God's ways. As we parted, I thanked him for his concern and told him he spoke beautiful words, and I would try to remember them.

I did take a minute to point out to him that up home, being in the Maine woods every day, I interact with God not only on the Sabbath, but on the other six days of the week as well. I told him that any location at all would be a place of worship of my choosing, it being a beautiful part of God's creation that I found to be much more inspirational than the inside of a building where one sat on a bench for an hour once a week. One cannot spend even a moment in the Maine woods without realizing that God's ways and works are everywhere. As he shook my hand to say goodbye, he said, "You are a very interesting person."

As a young boy, I enjoyed wandering off all alone and climbing to the top of Saddleback Mountain to visit the forest ranger who manned the forest fire look-out tower on the summit. He pointed out to me that on certain clear days, looking to the west, he could see the smoke from the cog railway on Mount Washington in New Hampshire. Also, looking northerly, he could see Mount Katahdin; and, southerly, the ocean off the coast of Maine. It is a known fact that the first land that is seen by ships on the ocean approaching Maine is Mount Blue, which I could never understand because Saddleback Mountain is taller. Since that time, I have spent many hours of my life sitting on the summit of Saddleback Mountain, gazing at the beauty one sees in all of the four directions.

One of the times I was sitting there, I became a little depressed by my ignorance of God's work, as compared to most people. Actually, about the only thing I knew about God's work was, "He created the Earth in six days, and on the seventh day He rested." All of a sudden, it sort of dawned on me that I might know something about God's work that no one else knew. I believe I know what He did on the eighth day:

The Eighth Day

On the eighth day,
God arose from His rest
and wandered over His creation,
gathering the best of His best.

From all His skies,
He took the bluest of blue
and selected a diamond sparkle
for His morning dew.

He searched His many waters
with care to be sure.
He gathered only the cool,
and only the pure.

He placed harbors and beaches
with the finest white sand,
fenced with a rocky coast,
where the sea meets the land.

Between His majestic mountains,
He placed valleys with rich soil,
so we would know rewards
for a long day's toil.

Then using essence of balsam
He aromatized the trees,
its fragrance carried afar,
by the constant mountain breeze.

So, by gathering the best of the best
from His great domain,
on the eighth day,
God created Maine!

Steve Bean.

BORN TO FLY

The passing away of a close friend or loved one leaves a hole in the heart that takes a long time to heal. The pain never completely goes away. I am from a family of 12 children—11 brothers and sisters. I have seen 10 of them pass on. It's hard to talk about a person after they have passed, but it needs to be done to be sure they are not forgotten. I can't recall someone's death without recalling at least part their lives as well.

I think of the many stories, poems, songs, or ballads of those who passed that help keep their memory alive. Little Joe the Wrangler, a cowboy killed by a stampede during a cattle drive. The logger killed in a logjam at Gerry's Rocks. The daring heroics of an infantry soldier, Roger Young. A tombstone every mile of truckers driving the Haynesville Woods of Maine. These lyrics help make sure their lives are never forgotten.

I recall hearing my grandfather telling my father that he believed when a person dies they die three times. The first time is when their heart stops beating. The second time is when they are buried or cremated. The third time is when their name is spoken for the last time. If their name is not spoken for the last time, their spirit will live on and on and will never be forgotten.

On December 22 in the year 2000, three days before Christmas, the gaiety and spirit of the Yuletide season in the community of Rangeley was shattered by the sudden death of its well-known and loved member Stephen Albert Bean, a best of the best pilot who lost his life in a plane crash. He was approaching his hometown of Rangeley, and it's known the airport was in sight, but what is not known is why the crash happened. After several investigations, the answer still remains unknown.

Those who knew Steve would agree he lived his life pretty much the way the Good Lord intended, with care and concern for his community as well as his country. His love and devotion for his wife and soulmate, Joann, and their lovely daughter, Judy, was second to none—with Judy being proof that the apple doesn't fall far from the tree.

Steve was born with a passion for flying in his soul. While serving his country for four years in the United States Air Force, he received the Strategic Air Command Education Achievement Award. He was a commercial pilot with multi-engine, single-engine, and land and sea ratings. He was an FAA Flight Examiner and Instrument Flight Instructor and was a member of the FAA Safety Council. Commercial pilots from around the world would travel to Rangeley to get their sea plane flight training with Steve.

He was dedicated to sharing with people his passion for flying. His desire to fly and teach others of the sky enabled his dream of establishing the Mountain Air Service to become a reality. With over 20,000 hours in the air—equivalent to every single minute in a span of three years, he became recognized as one of the greatest bush pilots in the Northeast.

Written in the annals of those born to fly, Steve's name will always remain at the top. And, it is fitting that a quote of Leonardo da Vinci is inscribed on his stone: "When once you have tasted flight, you will forever walk the Earth with your eyes turned skyward, for there you have been and there you will always long to return." If angels in Heaven are trained to fly before receiving their wings, it is now done in Heaven as it was on Earth—trained by the best of the best, who once again is born to fly.

Born To Fly

In memory of Stephen A. Bean
Nov. 17, 1942 – Dec. 22, 2000

Learning comes for all
before taking to the sky.
Even the great eagle
once had to learn to fly.

Then comes the wisdom,
the rules of "how and why."
Now you are in control.
You're at home in the sky.

You dive, you glide, you soar.
You've mastered every test.
Oh! Born to fly! Born to fly!
You are now the best.

But "best" carries a burden.
And what you now must do
is teach others to fly
and become great like you.

As you follow your destiny,
teaching others of the sky,
you become a "King of Kings."
Born to fly! Born to fly!

Then so quickly and untimely
the silver lining drifts astray
and a terrible tragedy
happens along your way.

No one seems to know
what happened, they say,
as to why your plane
came down that way.

But deep inside I believe
could be a reason why—
God called home His best
to teach angels to fly.

And as I walk this land,
I glance upwards to the sky.
I still sense your being
once again "Born To Fly."

Evergreen Cemetery, Rangeley.

Long, hard winters in Rangeley, Maine.

WINTER BLUES

The State of Maine is known for its severe winters. History tells us the year of 1816 in Maine was known as "1816 and froze to death." The Native Americans referred to it as "The year with no summer." Every month of the year had snow, frosts, and below-freezing temperatures. The settlers of that time could grow no crops, so many of them hitched up their wagons and moved to the Ohio River Valley, seeking a warmer clime.

Over the years, Maine winters have tamed a little bit, but old-fashioned winters are still common, especially in the mountains of the Rangeley Lakes Region where the average annual snowfall for Saddleback Mountain is over 200 inches. Snowfalls of three or four feet at a time still happen, with temperatures dropping to 30 or 40 degrees below zero for days at a time. I still remember the January day in 1958 when many thermometers in Rangeley read 48 below zero. Rangeley winters usually arrive just after Halloween and leave around the first of May, making them quite lengthy.

In my growing-up days, the old folks took their preparations for winter quite seriously. Barns were filled with hay, woodsheds filled with firewood, and cellars filled with a store of enough nourishing foods to last six months. A typical cellar had some vegetables hanging from the ceiling by their tops, just as they were pulled from the garden. Others were home-canned, along with pickles and preserves that filled many shelves. The most important was a wooden bin filled with the mainstay staple of potatoes, along with another bin for apples. For those who went all the way, a large, wooden barrel of cider was set to harden for making Applejack or just for sipping during the long storytelling evenings.

A tradition I'll always remember—Groundhog Day, what the old folks called Candlemas Day—was celebrated as much as Thanksgiving or Christmas. For, be it by calendar only, it did represent the half-way mark of winter. Families in the neighborhood took stock of all their supplies to see if they had half of everything left to finish the winter. If someone had extra hay but not enough firewood and someone else had extra firewood but not enough hay, a swap was made. If someone had extra potatoes but not enough vegetables and someone else had extra vegetables but not enough potatoes, another swap was made. It was a custom of neighbor helping neighbor. I recall a little ditty my father and grandfather used to sing:

>Groundhog Day
>Groundhog Day
>Half my taters
>Half my hay
>Half my cider peed away!

Today's advancements in wintertime activities such as skiing, snowboarding, ATVing, and snowmobiling make winters pass more quickly for many, but for those who have lived them, old-time Rangeley winters can still bring the blues.

Winter Blues

>The sun goes down,
>another day is through.
>A cold winter day,
>leaving me blue.
>
>Water-ways are frozen,
>harsh north winds blow.
>God's fields and forests
>wear a blanket of snow.

No grass of green,
no morning birds' song.
Why, oh why, does
winter last so long?

Nights grow longer,
stealing hours from day.
Melancholy sets in.
Please winter, go away!

I pray for patience,
for this too shall pass.
Spring will again come.
Forever, winter can't last.

Let me not forget
summer flowers grow
from seeds in waiting
beneath the deep snow.

Dead wood.

NATURE'S WAY

Many professionals such as guides, loggers, and sportsmen are often referred to as woodsmen, but that label is misleading and not always in conformity with truth. A true woodsman is not just aware of his surroundings but is also attuned to the elements and understands the forces of Mother Nature.

My father and his father were true woodsmen and often told me no college can provide a degree for being a woodsman. Being a true woodsman can only come from living a lifetime in the woods or having the woods born in him. Both of these sources attest to my authenticity as a true woodsman.

While growing up, much of my woods lore came from hunting and fishing—not as a sport but out of necessity, providing food to survive. At the time, fish and game, along with many of nature's edible greens, were major food staples. While gathering from the land, my father used to say, "Learn while you earn." If you gather a supply of fiddlehead greens, pay attention to where, when, and how they grow. To be successful at bagging fish and game, know the nature and habits of all wildlife.

A woodsman understands Mother Nature's role in balancing the life of all living things in the forest, including the trees, and accepts what cannot be changed. Having worked many years in the woods as a logger, I have been responsible for the death of many trees. Each death was balanced by the tree's new life as a commodity that serves civilization. As the tree dies, it leaves behind its seed to grow a replacement.

The death of a tree by Mother Nature seems to follow no rules other than the survival of the fittest. Regardless of age, quality, or species, a tree gets uprooted and dies, only to lie in state on the forest floor as dead wood. A woodsman in tune with the ways of nature sees a hidden beauty in its remains, turns it into a treasure, and the dead wood lives on.

Nature's Way

As wildlife stirs,
birds sing their song.
In the deep woods,
a tree is born.
From a fallen seed
of a towering pine,
a new life begins
in a new time.
    It is nature's way

Embedded in rich soil
of the forest's floor,
nursed by nature,
life starts to soar.
As time goes by,
the tree grows tall,
and its own seeds
start to fall.
    It is nature's way

Suddenly, without warning,
nature's wild side shows.
Torrential rains, fierce winds
with smothering snows—
all create a Hell on Earth.
When the storms subside,
long before its time,
a young tree has died.
    It is nature's way

The tree now lies
on the forest's floor.
Its remains are preserved,
but grows no more—
becoming seasoned and polished
in ways only nature could—
and awaits a new life
as a jewel of wood.
    It is nature's way

Then along comes man,
a true woodsman is he,
with an eye for beauty
that most can't see.
Retrieving the dead tree,
forgiving nature's wrong,
he creates a treasure
and dead wood lives on.
    This is a woodsman's way

Racks for clothes and more, in different stages of completion, made by Jeep Wilcox, using dead wood.

Maine Moose Meet.

NOAH'S MISTAKE

Of all the animals in the animal kingdom, I believe the most ugly and stupid of all is the moose. I think when God made the animals, He made the moose last, using leftover parts from other animals. It appears He took the body of a buffalo, put on the legs of a giraffe, the head of a horse, with ears from a donkey, big eyes from an alligator, a beard from a goat, and a little tail from a sheep. Wow! No wonder it's so ugly.

And stupid! A moose will stand beside a road and watch a car coming fifty miles an hour then step right out in front of it. Now that is dumb! If it gets away with it unharmed, it's apt to do the same thing time and time again. Oh, stupid moose!

Statistics tell us there are 70,000 to 80,000 moose in the State of Maine. The only state with more is the State of Alaska, which is much larger in acreage. Many of the moose in Maine make the Rangeley Lakes Region their home, drawing hundreds of visitors just to see one. Moose are so plentiful that Route 16, connecting Rangeley to the neighboring village of Eustis only 19 miles away, is known as "Moose Alley." Under the right conditions, an evening drive along "Moose Alley" will allow one to see 25 or 35 moose along the way, giving a large boost to tourism.

I have often wondered why there are so many more moose in the State of Maine. Why aren't there more of them out in the Midwestern states where the big corn and wheat fields are, or up in Montana where the buffalo and antelope roam? And then I recalled a story from the Good Book.

The story tells us that near the beginning God got quite frustrated with how things were going in the beautiful world He created, and decided it needed a good cleansing. So, He made it rain for many days and nights and flooded the whole Earth. He selected Noah and his family to be saved, and instructed him to build an ark and put aboard two of all the animals—one of each sex—and after the flood was over, turn them loose on land, and let them multiply. Being the loyal servant Noah was, he built the Ark, loaded the animals, and rode out the flood. Being so exhausted, he slept through it all. The story tells that after many days of rest, Noah awoke; the rain had stopped, and a dove swooped down with a twig from an olive branch in its beak, alerting Noah that land was near—which he soon saw. The flood waters were receding, leaving the Ark on land. He turned the animals loose with a feeling of mission accomplished.

Now, I wouldn't doubt a story from the Good Book, but I wonder if a mistake or two in its telling might have been made, and it went more like this:

Noah's Mistake

The Lord summoned Noah
in the middle of the night.
He said, "Build an ark,
and build it just right.

"When you have finished,
what I want you to do next
is load two of all my animals,
one of each sex.

"When I stop the rain
and let my new world dry,
you turn them loose on land,
and they will multiply.

"Now listen carefully, Noah,
for I made a mistake.
There is one of my animals
I don't want you to take.

"I made it from leftover parts
late one night.
I made it ugly and stupid.
It's a horrible sight.

"In the beauty of my new world
it will have no use,
so I want you to leave behind
my ugly, stupid moose."

Well, Noah worked hard
for many a day and night.
Like the Good Lord ordered,
he built the Ark just right.

Just as he was lowering
the ramp to the ground,
the heavy rains
came pouring down.

Knowing that the land
would soon be gone,
Noah opened the corral gate
and loaded the animals on.

He said, "Get aboard, camel.
On you go, pig.
Up the ramp, elephant.
Wow, you're big!

"Get aboard, tiger.
On you go, cow.
Get moving, pokey donkey.
Hurry up now.

"Get aboard, lion.
Up the ramp, goat.
Oh, don't worry.
It will float."

Noah got the animals loaded,
along with food and hay.
As the land disappeared,
the Ark sailed away.

Now, Noah was exhausted
from his hard-working ways,
so he took a nap
that lasted several days.

When he awoke from
his much-needed rest,
there was a crow
perched on his chest.

In the crow's beak,
wiggling with a squirm,
from land somewhere
was a fresh earthworm.

Then Noah saw that land.
He said, "It's just as well,
cause this ole Ark
is beginning to smell."

So he lowered the ramp
beneath the bright, sunny sky.
He said, "Go forth, animals.
Have fun and multiply.

"Off you go, horse.
So long, raccoon.
Be on your way,
you funny baboon.

"Come on down, bear.
Get going, you silly goose.
Down the ramp,
you ugly, stupid moose."

"Uh-oh!" Noah said. "I made a mistake!"

But God said, "It's okay, Noah.
I'll forgive you this time.
To err is human;
to forgive, divine.

"Put that ugly, stupid moose
back on the Ark again.
Then turn it loose
on the coast of Maine.

"Once and for all,
it will have a use—
drawing visitors from afar
to see my ugly, stupid moose."

THE LYING MOUNTAIN LION

Whatever you choose to call it—mountain lion, cougar, panther, or puma, does the mountain lion exist in the Maine woods today? Experts, such as biologists and environmentalists, say no, but the many people who spend hours nearly every day in the Maine woods—such as guides, hikers, sportsmen, and, particularly, loggers—disagree. What do you believe?

It seems that the so-called experts on wildlife in the Maine woods are more inclined to believe that Bigfoot—the Sasquatch—roams the Maine woods than they are to believe that a mountain lion does.

It is interesting to note that people once doubted that coyotes lived in the Maine woods. The late Gene Letourneau, though, a well-loved and respected veteran reporter who wrote the *Portland Press Herald* column "Sportsmen Say" for nearly 60 years, long maintained that coyotes were here. An undisputed authority on wildlife in the Maine woods, Letourneau spent nearly 30 years verifying that coyotes existed in Maine. For 50 years, the so-called experts reacted with skepticism, but now everyone agrees that there are thousands of coyotes roaming the Maine woods in packs. In fact, the number of coyotes appears to have contributed to the decline in the Maine deer herd.

In 1995, after many years of mountain lion sightings reported by reliable eye-witnesses in nearly every county of the State of Maine, the first scientifically verified sighting of a mountain lion in the Maine woods since 1938 was put on the books; but, the experts still say—now, over 20 years later—that no population of mountain lions exists in Maine today. They say the mountain lions are just passing through.

Does history repeat itself? Who knows? Maybe the mountain lion population in the Maine woods will multiply enough and chase the coyotes back out West. It would seem there are times when seeing things that are not supposed to exist are best explained by logic:

The Lying Mountain Lion

I was near the top of the mountain.
Feeling weary I sat down
by the entrance to a cave.
There were boulders all around.

Jumping up in front of me
by the cave where I sat—
I saw what I thought, surely
was the world's biggest cat.

It let out an ungodly scream
that made my hair stand on end.
Just like in the story of Daniel,
I'd wandered into a lion's den.

Its whiskers and little pointy ears
and long tail it kept flicking about
assured me it was a mountain lion.
Of that there was no doubt.

Unwise to a lion's ways,
my body filled with fear.
So I sent a message down to my feet—
"Hurry! Get me out of here!"

Just a few days later,
as I was walking down the street,
a State of Maine game warden
I happened by chance to meet.

As I told of what I saw,
I was stunned by words he did say—
"There are no mountain lions
in these Maine woods today!"

Well now, I saw what I saw.
Of that there is no denying.
So it comes quite clear to me—
someone around here is lying.

Now, of course, we all know
a game warden wouldn't lie.
And I couldn't tell a tall tale,
no matter how I try.

So the next time I see that lion,
I'll close my eyes so I can't see,
for it's a lying mountain lion,
trying to make a liar out of me!

Left to right: Loggers Robert Wilcox, his cousin Everett Wilcox, and another man whose name is unknown. 1943.

THE LOGGER WHO CUTS THE TREE

The landmass within the borders of the State of Maine totals just over 20 million acres. Setting aside the acreage that is not tree covered, Maine still has just under 18 million acres of tree-covered land. The only state in the United States that has more trees than Maine is the State of Alaska, which has a much larger landmass. Maine, known as the "Pine Tree State" in the great "North Woods," is the most heavily forested state in the United States. A large portion of its nearly 18 million acres of trees lies in Maine's western mountains, with the Rangeley Lakes Region having the most dense forestland in the State. The land in Down East Maine is noted for the seemingly endless blueberry barrens that provide the blueberries that Maine is famous for. The land in the northern part of the State, in the Saint John's River Valley, has many miles of flat, rolling potato fields that Maine is also famous for.

The Rangeley Lakes Region has a very rich history of logging that should never be forgotten, for it was the major way of life long before the tourists came. The railroads were built for logging; the tourists came after. Logging still goes on in a big way in the Region, although methods have changed over the years. Whether it was old-time logging—done with horses, axes, bucksaws; loading and unloading trucks by hand power; and trucking logs to rivers to be floated and river-driven downstream to mills—or the modern-day methods with giant-sized logging equipment like skidders, forwarders, and harvesters—respect is still given to the original meaning of the word "logger," which refers to the man who cuts the tree down in the woods.

That's where it all starts, for if the logger didn't cut the tree, it couldn't be transported to the mills, made into paper, or sawed into lumber to build our homes. In fact, before Noah built the Ark, a logger cut the tree. Logging is a very necessary part of life on Earth today; and if you object to logging, just try using plastic toilet paper!

The Logger Who Cuts The Tree

Did you ever stop to think
what a different world this would be
if it wasn't for the logger,
the one who cuts the tree?

Missing would be many means
to earn a livelihood.
Missing would be the beauty
of a finished piece of wood.

Our homes would be steel or stone,
for lumber there'd be none.
If it wasn't for the logger,
the sawmills couldn't run.

When the Lord summoned Noah,
as He planned our destiny—
yes, Noah built the Ark,
but a logger cut the tree.

Of course, trees make paper,
and lots of paper we need,
so a logger's job is important,
very important indeed.

For just think of the paper products
we take for granted every day—
books we read, the letters we write,
our checks when we get our pay.

But most of all—

If it wasn't for the logger,
the one who cuts the tree,
for the need of toilet tissue,
imagine what a crisis there'd be!

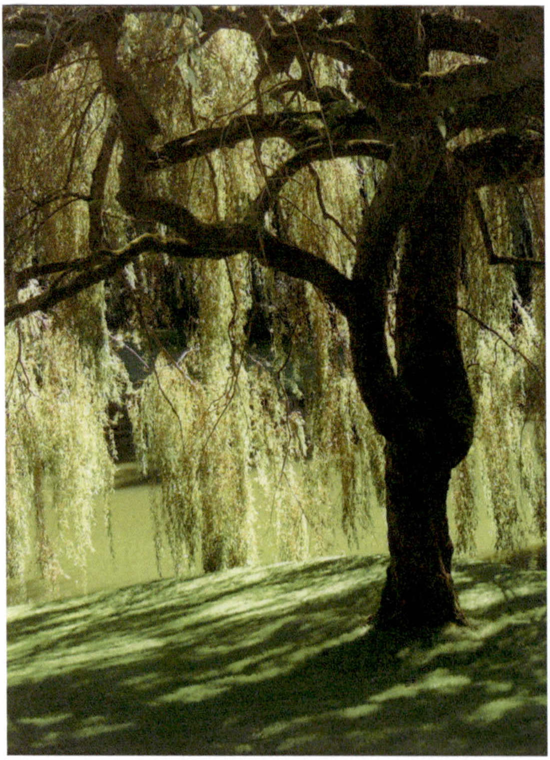

THE LEGEND OF THE WEEPING WILLOW

The creative power of imagination has brought much progress to civilization. It serves mankind in the world today and inspires the minds of those in the worlds of art and literature. As children, most of us have experienced fantasies of secret, invisible playmates, such as elves and fairies, or dolls and toys from Toyland that fantasy can make real. As we age, imagination allows us to envision everlasting life in the Kingdom of Heaven. Without imagination, there would be no dream-world, and dreams help make us what we are.

I can't write what I don't feel, and dreams hone my feelings. I have no control over my night dreams, but imagination gives free rein to my day dreams. I have always felt a sense of belonging in the deep woods among the trees, and I share a feeling of kinship with every tree in the forest. In my own imaginary way, it seems like the trees and I can communicate with each other. Had I lived a life in a different time long ago, I believe my Native American spiritual name might have been "Tree Talker" or "He Who Talks With Trees."

I recall the time I was returning from an all-day woods wandering, and I passed through a lush, green intervale with a pristine mountain brook flowing down the center—a scene right out of Disney World. As I crossed the brook, my eyes were drawn to a very large weeping willow tree growing on the bank. The tree was so huge I could not reach around it with both arms, and it had many twisted and gnarled limbs, covered with countless drooping leaves. My first thought was "What an ugly looking tree!"

It took me only a moment to realize how wrong I was. This weeping willow tree spoke to me of strength, wisdom, and everlasting life. I came to see that it was actually one of the most beautiful trees I have ever seen, and I realized that it had been around for a very long time. As I sat on the ground to gaze upon the beauty of this magnificent tree, these words came to me:

A Legend Of The Weeping Willow Tree

I sat for a while today
'neath a weeping willow tree.
When I asked, "Why do you weep?"
it opened its heart to me.

It said, "I have been weeping
since a long time ago.
I can't count the reasons
that make my tears flow.

"I weep for our Saviour
who died upon the cross.
I weep for many souls,
wandering or lost.

"I weep for the homeless,
the sick, and the old.
I weep for broken hearts
from love that's grown cold.

"I weep for pollution
rivers carry to the sea.
I weep for the blind
who can't see what you see.

"I weep for those who give all
so others remain free.
I weep for a world so divided,
united 'twill never be.

"Of countless reasons I weep.
The one that tortures me
is there will always be a need
for the Weeping Willow Tree."

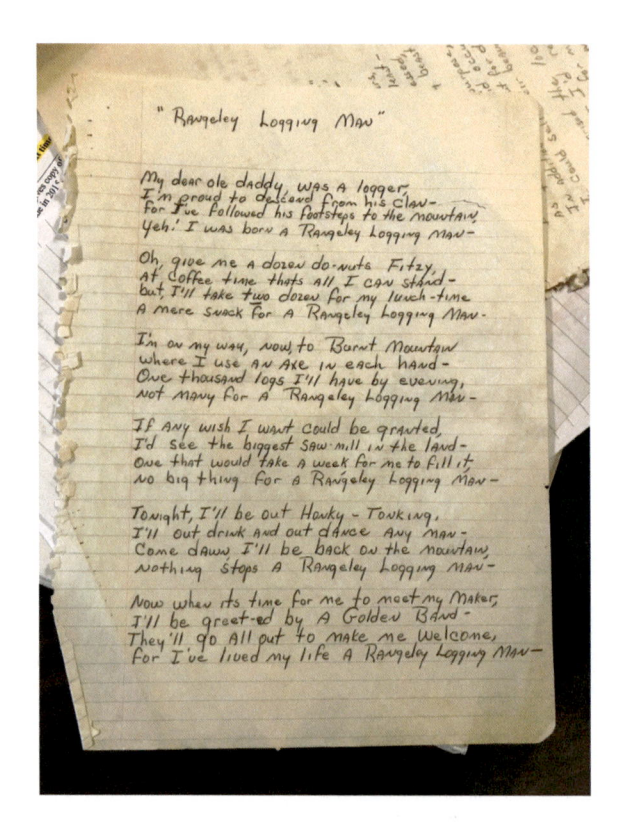

*One of Jeep's poems that hung on the bulletin board of D.C. Morton's
Texaco station, laid out on Jeep's dining room table
as Jeep and Peggy worked on this book.*

LOCAL ENTERTAINMENT CENTER

The town of Rangeley is well-known for its many tourists and visitors who come and go and are welcomed with open arms, but the locals who make up the core of the population, who rub elbows with each other on a daily basis, provide a closeness like family. Not only are they concerned with each other's health and welfare, but also they pray together in church, cry together at funerals, and laugh together at each other's humorous downfalls.

It is typical of small rural towns in Maine to have a favorite spot that locals tend to gather in the daily routine of their lives. Maybe a post office where "Good morning" greetings are passed on, or a coffee shop or general store for catching up on current events, or the much-needed gas station that cares for their automotive needs—becoming a sort of headquarters.

In days gone by, before gas stations all became self-service, Rangeley was blessed with a gas station known as D. C. Morton and Sons Texaco Station that was the pride of the State of Maine and was the focal point of local activity. A tradition created by founder Donald "Bart" Morton and carried on by sons Donnie and Dick—full service was given. With a purchase of gas, the customer received a tire pressure check, an oil check, and a washed windshield at no extra charge, as well as a genuine "How are you today?"—bringing to mind the friendly atmosphere of Goober pumping gas at Wally's garage in the town of Mayberry.

The well-known gentleman who pumped the gas at D.C. Morton's Texaco Station was also the local undertaker. In addition to the friendly service, there were several chairs in the lobby of the office, arranged around a never-empty coffee urn, allowing folks to sit and swap a few words of wisdom with each other.

Nearby, mounted on the wall, was a bulletin board for postings of local affairs and events, and many were the topic of conversation.

After an amusing story-poem that I wrote was displayed on the bulletin board by an employee—it started with the lines

> Our world has many problems
> but one thing I want to know:
> Who undertakes the undertaker
> when it's his turn to go?

people were constantly stopping by to read many poems about local happenings that were posted under the heading of "Jeep's Stories of the Week." Here are a few of them:

Rangeley Logging Man

My dear old daddy was a logger,
I'm proud to descend from his clan,
for I've followed his footsteps to the mountain—
Yeah! I was born a Rangeley Logging Man.

Oh, give me a dozen donuts, Fitzy.
At coffee time, that's all I can stand.
But I'll take two dozen for my lunch-time—
A mere snack for a Rangeley Logging Man.

If any wish I want could be granted,
I'd see the biggest sawmill in the land,
one that would take a week for me to fill it—
No big thing for a Rangeley Logging Man.

Tonight, I'll be out Honky-Tonking.
I'll out-drink and out-dance any man.
Come dawn, I'll be back on the mountain—
Nothing stops a Rangeley Logging Man.

Now, when it's time for me to meet my Maker,
I'll be greeted by a Golden Band.
They'll go all out to make me welcome,
for I've lived my life a Rangeley Logging Man.

The Devil's Machine

From the center of Hell
where the Devil was born,
there is no doubt about it—
they named him John.

And without hesitation
he achieved his goal.
He created a way
to torture man's soul.

He threw together a machine
that wouldn't last a year.
Instead of John Devil,
he called it a John Deere!

The cost of the machine
is only the start.
In no time at all,
you'll replace every part.

A fool and his money
are parted, I hear.
Just ask anyone
who owns a John Deere!

It will take all your money,
besides what you've spent,
and leave your mind fractured,
twisted, and bent.

For two things go together,
more than baseball and beer—
It's a goddamned fool
and a machine by John Deere!

In all of "God's" Earth,
there is only one sin
for which there is no pardon—
so never give in.

That's when a man's mind
starts acting so queer
he even thinks
of buying a John Deere!

There is a bright side,
though it's a high price to pay.
It's a sure ticket to Heaven
when it comes Judgement Day.

For the sign on Heaven's Gate
reads "You're Welcome Here.
You've spent enough time in Hell,
if you owned a John Deere!"

John Devil Reforms?

I, John Devil,
hereby solemnly swear,
from now on,
to treat mankind fair.

I created a new machine,
so all goes well.
Nothing like the others
that I made in Hell.

A machine that is sturdy,
economical to run.
Compared to my others,
owning this one is fun.

Engineered to last longer
than man can live—
So come on, you contractors,
Let's forget and forgive.

I've worked hard
to give mankind belief
that I, John Devil,
turned over a new leaf.

My conscience has bothered.
I regret my past.
That's why I made a machine
which forever will last.

No more breakdowns.
Buy one, you've got it made.
Say nothing about
the money you'll have saved.

But best of all,
your mind will be clear,
if you buy a new machine
made by John Deere.

Big ones and small ones—
I have them any size.
It's my way of saying
that I apologize.

Yes, I've reformed.
I've now seen the light,
as I offer this machine
to show I can do right.

So, open your hearts
and, of course, your checkbook,
and buy a machine
with the new John Deere look.

Put your faith in me,
whatever you do,
and order yours today—
"You Sucker You!"

Blue Mack Blues

Now listen, all you truckers,
and hear what I say.
I will tell you what happened
down in Bemis one day.

Backing down a driveway
was the Morgan Mack Truck.
Quick as a bolt of lightning,
the Morgan Mack was stuck.

I hooked on the dozer.
With the winch, I gave a nudge.
Not a thing happened.
The Morgan Mack wouldn't budge.

"Give her some RPMs," I yelled,
"the better to help me."
Throwing the winch in gear,
I trigged the dozer with a tree.

Then I heard some strange words
flying through the air.
I looked around and saw it—
his drive shaft, laying there.

It took only a second
to see why Morgan looked so sick.
The shaft was all twisted.
It looked like a licorice stick.

I picked up the shaft, thinking,
for him, things don't look good.
I tell you true, you truckers,
that shaft was made of wood.

The universals on the end
had no sign of bolt or screw.
I could see they had been stuck on
with a bottle of Elmer's Glue.

Away he went in a hurry,
for time he was trying to save,
to a woodturning mill in Rumford.
They turned one out on a lathe.

I said, "Morgan, you should see Rodney.
He will treat you fair.
It will take only a moment
for him to whittle a spare.

"It would be a strong one.
He'll do a good job for you.
The cost will be reasonable,
for he'll throw in some glue.

"And as you keep on trucking,
this problem you'll have beat.
You will always have a spare
hidden under the seat."

Now, I tell all you truckers,
if you think of buying a Mack,
don't rush too quickly.
It might pay you to hang back.

Mack has a reputation
of making their trucks good,
but their drive shaft
is made out of wood!

The Wagon Wheel

Just outside of town,
there is a local spot
you really ought to try,
if you like your coffee hot.

Shirts and ties, or blue jeans—
come dressed the way you feel.
To Ralph and Kit, you're equal.
Welcome to The Wagon Wheel.

For be it a morning coffee
or an evening beer,
a snack or full course meal—
everyone is welcome here.

The aroma from the kitchen,
drifting through the air,
assures you home cooking
is truly mastered there.

Served by friendly people
with a pleasant smile,
at once you feel relaxed
and glad you stopped awhile.

So if you're eating out
and crave food that is real,
give yourself a treat—
stop at the Wagon Wheel.

Inside the Wagon Wheel, 1985.

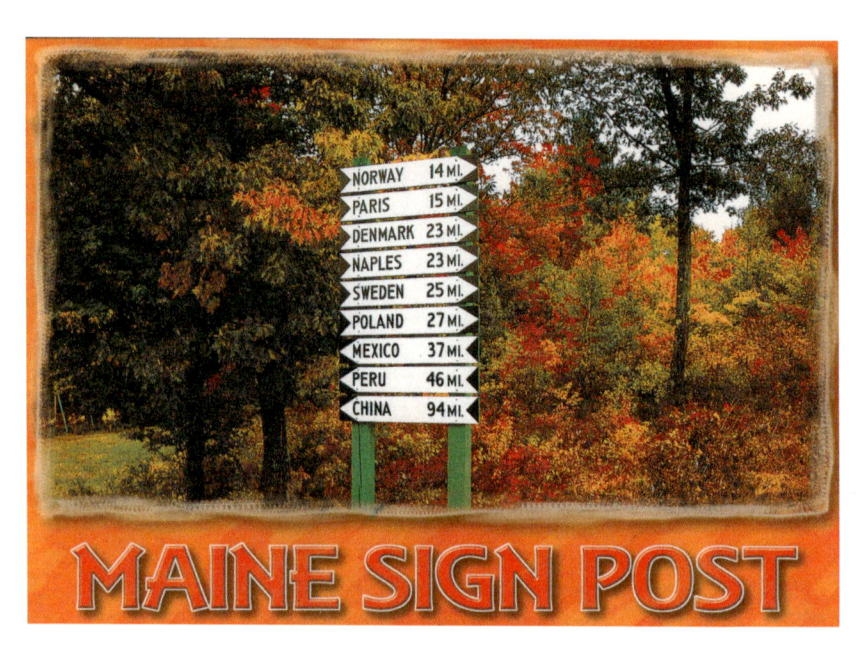

Signpost in Lynchville, Maine.

YOU CAN'T GET THERE FROM HERE, BUT YOU CAN GET HERE FROM THERE

A couple of good storytellers that teamed up together to tell some very humorous "taste of Maine" stories were the late Marshall Dodge and his very good friend Robert Bryan. Many years ago, they got together and created the two now very well-known characters of "Bert and I." Along with these stories that "Bert and I" told were the sound effects they used, which are totally unbelievable. Whether it is the sound of a lobster boat pulling into the harbor or the sound of a chain saw cutting a tree, anyone sitting inside of a building hearing these sounds coming in through an open window would swear the real thing was outside, even if there were no ocean or trees in the area.

Now, Marshall and Bob did their job so well that anyone who listened to "Bert and I" began to envision them as real people. Of course they did! That's what real storytellers do: make believers out of their listeners. Then again, maybe Marshall and Bob were only portraying themselves.

Out of all the many stories "Bert and I" told, the most famous one of all that will never be forgotten—and if it didn't put Maine on the map, it sure as hell spread Maine's fame all across the country—is that of "I" having a little fun giving travel directions to some tourists seeking a small town in Maine that they couldn't find.

These tourists spied "I" standing outside a grocery store, and they stopped and asked him, "Can you tell us how to get to that town?" So, he gave the people from away some very confusing up and down and over directions. And then, he finally said, "Come to think of it, you can't get there from here!"

Now this quote really caught on and spread far and fast. Everyone was laughing and saying, "Can't get there from here."

These words came to depict the State of Maine as much as, if not more than, the moose, lobster, or pine tree. Everyone was joking about it, and people from away took it back to their hometowns and states: "Up in Maine, you can't get there from here." It got so popular that it sort of became a slogan or a logo for business people, and it spread far beyond the New England States.

Well, I had just finished telling a few stories myself at The Maine Festival one year; and on the long drive home, I got to thinking about ole "Bert and I." And it dawned on me—not only were these boys quite humorous, they were damn smart as well. The truth is, you can't get there from here.

That evening as I was sitting on my porch telling my neighbors who had dropped by all about the Festival, I pointed out how smart "Bert and I" really were. The whole country was laughing at "Bert and I" for telling "You can't get there from here," but they knew what they were talking about. You really can't get there from here.

But, "Bert and I" didn't tell all of it. The truth is, you can't get there from here, but you can get here from there.

Well, my company looked at me, and one said, "What's the matter with you, Jeep? What did you have to drink or smoke down there in the city? If you can't get there from here, how in the hell can you get here from there?" So, I explained:

You Can't Get There From Here, But You Can Get Here From There

Many people from our time
and some from yesteryear,
from all walks of life have tried,
but you can't get there from here.

It's been tried by the professor,
it's been tried by "Bert and I."
Even the astronauts tried it
from miles up in the sky.

It's been tried by the captain and navigator,
the pilgrim and the pioneer.
Even Einstein and Newton tried,
but you can't get there from here.

It's been attempted by the trucker,
the bus driver and the engineer.
Even the Maine Guides tried,
but you can't get there from here.

But for all who tried and failed,
be it by land, sea, or air,
in reverse they might have made it,
for you can get here from there.

It's really very simple,
which I'm sure you'll agree.
If you want to get here from there,
simply erase the "T."

If you don't get that right away, don't feel bad. I told that to a group of people at a Thanksgiving gathering one time, and as I was sitting down to my Christmas dinner, my phone rang. And when I answered, the guy on the other end was laughing and shouting and saying, "I got it, I got it!"

Sometimes it takes a while.

ACKNOWLEDGEMENTS

All photographs are by Gaylon "Jeep" Wilcox or courtesy of him, alone, with the exception of those listed below, in order of appearance in the book:

"The Fool's Gold" drawing by Jackie Myer, 2018.

"Man Made Lake" postcard photograph by Luther S. Phillips. Courtesy of Kenny Wing for the Flagstaff Memorial Chapel Association.

"Smokey's Home" photograph by Margaret Yocom, 2018.

"The Giving Tree" photograph by Kyle Haley Photography, khaleyphoto.com.

"School Inspirations: Tree To Table" photograph by Alison Loud, 2018. Courtesy of Alison Loud. With the permission of the Truland Family and the Sherrer Family.

"School Inspirations: Special People In Our Lives" photograph by Margaret Yocom, November 2018.

"School Inspirations: I See" photograph courtesy of Gaylon "Jeep" Wilcox and *The Rangeley Highlander*, where it first appeared in 1990.

"Walks of Life" postcard photograph by Lamson Studio, 1904. Courtesy of Rangeley Lakes Historical Society, Rangeley History Museum, Edward Ellis Postcard Collection, Album #2, Item #1997.006.0315.

"Seeing Is Believing" drawing by Jackie Myer, 2018.

"Born To Fly" photograph of Steve Bean and his airplane courtesy of Gaylon "Jeep" Wilcox and *The Rangeley Highlander* where it appeared on 17 January 2001, p. 15.

"Deer Mountain Run" photograph by Margaret Yocom, previously published in *Working the Woods* by Yocom and Mundell, 1999.

"Lying Mountain Lion" drawing by Jackie Myer, 2018.

"You Can't Get There From Here, But You Can Get Here From There" postcard photograph by Lyman Owen, with the permission of Maine Scene Company of Union, Maine.

"Local Entertainment Center" photograph by Margaret Yocom, 2018.

"Rangeley Logging Man" photograph by Martha Cooper, previously published in Vermont Folklife Center's exhibit "Gather 'Round: Tales of New England's Work-A-Day World," 2000.

"The Devil's Machine" drawing by Jackie Myer, 2018.

"The Wagon Wheel" photograph by Margaret Yocom, 1985.

About the Editor photograph by Jamie Lynn Photography, jamielynnphoto.com.

About the Book quotation is found in Alfred R. Kitzhaber, general editor, *The Narrative Voice: Poetry*, p. ii (New York: Holt, Rinehart and Winston, 1974).

ABOUT THE AUTHOR

Jeep Wilcox grew up on a hardscrabble farm, the seventh of 12 children, and went to first through fifth grades in a one-room schoolhouse. He started creating story-poems at a very young age; the big woods of the Rangeley Lakes Region were his major inspiration. Born in him was a fascination for the woods so strong that when he was as young as five years old, his parents dared not leave him outside unattended for fear that he would wander off into the woods. By age 10, he was constantly roaming the Region's mountains and valleys like a sort of "Johnny Appleseed," leaving story-poems on trees by the waysides, using a pen, pencil, or jackknife.

His father often found him missing with his assigned chores left undone and remarked, "He's like one of those Jeeps, traveling down some old trail or logging tote road, off the beaten path." He would ask if anyone has seen "Jeep," a nickname that was instantly used by everyone and stuck for life.

As time passed, visitors and locals alike who used the same trails and tote roads while hiking, hunting, or fishing noticed the story-poems on the trees throughout the woods, and the story-poems became talked about by all. In his unique storytelling way, Jeep started sharing these story-poems with audiences of all kinds, unknowingly catching the attention of members of the Traditional Arts field and well-known folklorists; he found himself traveling down his own tote road of fame.

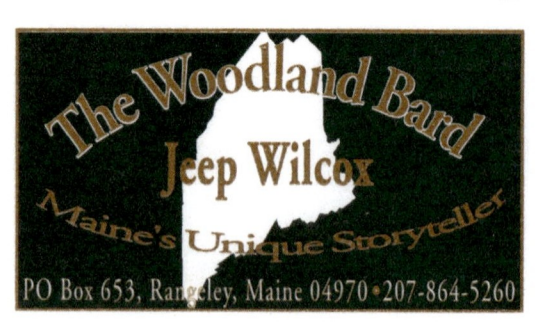

Critics have said that his performances are extraordinary—even flows of wit and philosophy that are very captivating. His road has led him to appearances at the Maine Folk Festival; the Lowell, Massachusetts, Folk Festival; the National Folk Festival in Bangor, Maine; the Northwest Folk Festival in Seattle, Washington; as well as at countless schools and civic organizations. He has been featured in documentaries, exhibits, and articles, including Peter Mehegen's "On the Road Again"; Public Broadcasting Service Radio; "Gather 'Round: Tales of New England's Work-A-Day World," an exhibit by the Vermont Folklife Center; and in several articles by folklorist Dr. Margaret Yocom, emerita, of George Mason University in Fairfax, Virginia. Over the years, he has shared his stories with tour bus visitors staying at the Rangeley Inn in his hometown of Rangeley, Maine; and he has now pleased audiences of more than 500 tour buses.

Jeep has worked as a logger, truck driver, and school custodian. From 1952 to 1956, during the Korean War era, he served in the U.S. Army Corps of Engineers. He helped build the largest jet base in England—Molesworth, and he received training in many wartime skills, including the handling of explosives.

Jeep's greatest joy is seeing the smiles and head nods of his nationwide story-poem listeners, for then he knows they are identifying with his ways and have formed a common-folk bond with him—and each other.

ABOUT THE EDITOR

Margaret "Peggy" Yocom grew up in the Pennsylvania German farmland listening to her grandparents' stories. Her book *ALL **KINDS** OF **FUR**: Erasure Poems & New Translation of a Tale from the Brothers Grimm* was published by Deerbrook Editions in 2018. Her poetry has also appeared in the *Beloit Poetry Journal*, *The Beltway Poetry Journal*, the anthology *The Folklore Muse: Poetry, Fiction, and Other Reflections by Folklorists*, and elsewhere. She founded the Folklore Studies Program of George Mason University where she taught for 36 years; among her many courses, she offered "Living Words: Folklore and Creative Writing." For her work at the University, the American Folklore Society awarded her the Kenneth Goldstein Award for Lifetime Academic Leadership. She has published on the Brothers Grimm, on the folk arts of political protest, on Inuit storytelling in northwest Alaska, on family folklore, and on the folk arts of Maine logging communities, especially on the Rodney Richard Family of Rangeley. From 1975 until 2014, she helped the Richards with the Rangeley Lakes Region Logging Museum that they founded, serving as volunteer and curator. Co-founder of the American Folklore Society's Creative Writing and Storytelling Section, she holds a Ph.D in English and Folklore from the University of Massachusetts at Amherst. A founding member of Western Maine Storytelling, she tells legendary tales of the seen—and the unseen. Co-organizer of the Hugh Ogden Memorial Evening of Poetry in Rangeley, she makes her home with her geologist husband, John Slack, in Farmington and Rangeley. http://margaretyocom.com

FROM THE EDITOR

It has been my very great pleasure to work with Jeep on his book of story-poems. He and I began talking about this project from the time we met in Rangeley in 1985. Through many folk festivals, hikes up Saddleback, rides along the back roads, and hours of talk, our friendship grew—and continues to grow. Jeep's story-poems help tell the cultural history of his hometown from his unique perspective, and I am honored to have a part in getting them into print for the delight of others, especially his Rangeley neighbors.

Everything you read in this book is written by Jeep. I worked with him on multiple drafts of the story-poems, typed everything, scanned the images, helped him decide on the book's final shape, and served as his liaison to Höhne-Werner Design. I suggested additions, deletions, and changes in spelling, punctuation, word choice, and more; and Jeep has had the final say in almost all decisions. All opinions and stated facts in this book are, likewise, his. Thanks to Höhne-Werner Design of Wilton for following Jeep's wishes, as well. All proceeds from this book go to Jeep and his family.

I dedicate my work to Jeep and his family, and, as ever, to my husband, Dr. John F. Slack, for his constant support—and, for his help with proofreading.